Shirley,

Grace & peace
to you.

Joan

BEHOLD!
BORN UNTO YOU
'The Story Between
The Verses'

By: Joan M. Geisler

Published by

G Cubed Productions

Fredericksburg, Virginia USA

beholdbornuntoyou.com

Printed in the USA

ISBN: **978-0-9896843-0-9**

ISBN-13: **978-0-9896843-0-9**

CONTENTS

Reviews of "BEHOLD! Born Unto You"

Remaining true to scriptural accuracy, Joan imaginatively captures each personality while introducing the reality of everyday life and real human responses to the sacred event that changed the course of human history. I was captivated and inspired by the retelling of this beautiful story.   Marilyn Wood

I hadn't thought very deeply "between the lines" of the nativity story in Scripture before. Joan took me deeper into life for Mary and Joseph. What a thought-provoking story! God has truly gifted Joan in her writing.   Robin Woodard

Just as Cecil B DeMille filled in the "story between the verses" in his epic movie, The Ten Commandments, and the story of Moses, so too does Joan Geisler in her new book, "Behold, Born Unto You", and the story of the birth of Jesus. No doubt destined to be a Christmas classic.   Kelly Gebert

ACKNOWLEDGEMENTS

Thanks be to God who has blessed me with every spiritual blessing in the heavenly places in Christ. Ephesians 1:3

Among His greatest blessings to me is my husband Gary. We have been a terrific team since our marriage in 1989. God blessed us with four children; Austin, Isaac, Gretchen and Phoebe. They are the joy of our lives.

I am also blessed to have been raised in a large family who love and support each other. Thank you Karla, Julie, Kurt, Kristin, Jayne, Kelly, Jean and my remarkable mother, Helen. Our father, Ray, has gone to be with the Lord.

Thank you to all who previewed my rough drafts and gave me the encouragement to pursue my dream of writing; Becky Turner, Robin Woodard, Vivian West and Diane Johnson.

I believe God inspired me to write this book and then gave me a talented editor, Marilyn Wood, to bring my thoughts and grammar together.

Special thanks to Heshmat Mirsepasi of Royal Hair Studio and Linda Strand of Winterberry Portraits for making my photograph so beautiful.

I pray this book will bring glory to God.

This book is dedicated to our great God who demonstrated His own love for us in this;

"While we were still sinners, Christ died for us."

Romans 5:8

Therefore, half of the proceeds from the sale of this book will go to furthering the Kingdom of God.

We invite you to visit our website beholdbornuntoyou.com and leave a comment or a review.

The beautiful cover entitled "Silent Night" was painted by Liz Lemon Swindle. She, too, thought that Joseph had a bigger role in the birth and raising of Jesus than scripture reveals. Her portrayal of Joseph and mine are of the same mind. I am privileged to have her painting represent my book. You can view more of Ms. Swindle's work at lizlemonswindle.com

INTRODUCTION

God's Word Made Alive

Have you ever wondered about the story of the nativity, the birth of Jesus Christ? Most people know the story. They read or hear it once a year at Christmas time and take it at face value and move on to the shopping and gift-giving which the season demands. Those who have heard it could give a quick synopsis of the story. An angel visits a young girl named Mary and then her fiancé' Joseph. They go to Bethlehem where they find no room at the inn and stay in a manger, a barn. Jesus is born, shepherds from the fields and wise men from the east come and worship the baby wrapped in swaddling clothes and lying in a manger. This is a very beloved story people read year after year after year.

BUT

Have you ever thought about what happened in between the verses? I saw a picture years ago of Joseph holding the baby in the foreground and Mary resting on a blanket in the hay in the background. Joseph is looking at the baby like all new fathers do, counting the fingers and toes and gazing at this miracle of birth. It made me wonder what really happened during the story of Christ's birth. Was it really a "Silent Night"? Holy night, yes, but there were a lot of animals in that barn and a lot of people milling around Bethlehem for it to be a 'silent night.' 'Oh little town of Bethlehem how still we see thee lie." I don't think it was still either. And who said it was just a few shepherds? Why were there not several of them? Who said there were only three wise men? They probably traveled with a huge entourage. The text of the Bible clearly indicates that the wise men did not find Mary and the baby in the manger. Matthew 2:11 says "On coming to the house, they saw the child with his mother Mary, and they bowed down and worshiped him." Now a manger would never be called a house, so it is clear that the wise men were not at the manger scene. And Luke 2:39 says, "When Joseph and Mary had done everything required by the Law of the LORD, they returned to Galilee to their own town of Nazareth." So they did not take up residence in Bethlehem. They headed back home, so the wise men must have found them in Nazareth. I know all those songwriters were taking poetic liberties just like I am about to do. But I still wonder at the real story.

Have you ever stopped to think about the cast of characters?

The people involved were real people with real stories.

Mary was a young girl who chatted with her girlfriends, had crushes on boys, learned to cook and clean, and dreamed of her future husband.

Joseph was a man who worked hard for a living. He was taught the trade of a carpenter, as was his father before him. He had friends, joked around, and worked hard to build a life for himself and his future wife.

Elizabeth and Zachariah were real people. They carried enormous grief over Elizabeth's barrenness. They worked, probably gardened, had friends and served in the temple.

They all were normal people just like you and I. They all loved the LORD with all their hearts but were sinful like we all are and allowed their anger and frustrations to get the best of them at times.

I write this book with tremendous reverence toward God. I am so thankful that God inspired Matthew and Luke to record this story. I am so thankful that God had a redemption plan. I like to look at the Bible as a whole. Starting with Genesis, it opens with "In the beginning God created the heavens and the earth." God made the world and then filled it with fabulous oceans and mountains to be explored, lush greenery for our aromatic senses, exotic flowers and animals for our visual delight and foods of all variety to encounter to our heart's content.

And then He created two people to live in this paradise and to start the human race.

Unfortunately this did not seem to be enough for Adam and Eve. They disobeyed and brought sin into the world.

Thus God put His plan into action to send a Savior into the world to redeem mankind from the fallen state of sin. *"Just as sin entered the world through one man, and death through sin, and in this way death came to all men, because all sinned."*

Romans 5:12.

This Savior had to be born without this strain of sin flowing through

His veins. He had to be sinless. Only God is sinless: therefore God had to be the father of this Savior. Better yet, God BECAME the Savior. God did not 'create' His Son, like God created the world. Jesus was with God from the beginning of time. The Hebrew word for "God" is Elohim, which means a God with plural identities, like water can be frozen, steam or liquid, each one serving a different purpose. God is Jesus, Jesus is God. God is the Holy Spirit. God became the Son and sent Himself to earth to die for the sins of mankind. God *became flesh and dwelt among us,* John 1:14, so He can identify with our human weaknesses and frailties, Hebrews 10.

God left His heavenly throne and was born a helpless baby to a virgin girl. Yes, God could have come as an adult man. But He had to experience life in the confinement of the human body so He can empathize with us. Hebrews chapter 9 and 10 explain all this.

I pray that you will enjoy this book and take it in the spirit with which it was written. I tried to put human life around the characters who participated in this most important time in history. It really happened. They were real people. I hope that it makes you appreciate God and what He did for us and that you draw closer to Him. I hope it makes you laugh and chuckle and causes an occasional tear as you read it, as it did to me.

It is the GREATEST story ever told.

Let's start at the beginning.

GENESIS 1:1 "IN THE BEGINNING GOD CREATED THE HEAVENS AND THE EARTH"

1

GOD

In the beginning, I, along with My Son and My Holy Spirit, created the heavens and the earth. We had a clean palate with which to start. The earth was dark and formless and My Spirit perched over it like an owl hovering over her young. Then I said, "*Let there be light.*" And KA BLAM!! My glory shown throughout all time and space.

We first divided the light from darkness and called it day and night. Then we divided the earth from the sky. We made the ground gather together and called it land, and the waters were gathered into different places, and We called them seas. We put boundaries around the seas to keep them in their places. We caused the seas to be a plethora of colors- the deepest turquoise in the Caribbean, emerald greens in the Mediterranean and steel gray of the cold north Atlantic Ocean. We made purple mountains of majesty, smoky-looking mountains, tall snow-covered Alps, volcanoes and rocky seaside cliffs. We made meadows and carpeted them in a blaze of colorful flowers and lush green pastures.

Then I said, "Let the earth sprout grasses, fruit trees that would yield seeds after their own kind, vegetables that would do the same, and beautiful flowers and trees that are almost too numerous to count. Variety has always been the spice of life. Don't you agree?"

We said to each other, "Now that looks great, this is good!" And We patted each other on the back. We did all that in just three days. But We were not finished.

It took Us just one more day to make the sun, moon, planets and all the myriad upon myriad of stars. We lined up the planets and placed them exactly in the atmosphere for which they were made. We put the stars in set shapes and patterns that will be called constellations, and We caused the moon to have a 30-day cycle of waxing and waning. We did that so when We created mankind they will be able to use the stars and moon to tell time and seasons and navigate the seas. Mankind will not discover for a very long time that the planets rotate around the sun and not the sun rotating around the planets. We have already chosen the scientist who will discover that mystery.

Now that there was food, water and sunlight on the earth, it was time to create something really interesting. ANIMALS!! OH MY! This was amusing and entertaining. We started with the basics, beaks, wings, snouts, tails, hooves, fur, and feathers. Then We formed fins, scales, gills, and blowholes. We molded itty-bitty insects that can hardly be detected and not so itty-bitty insects that are big and hairy and scary with long legs and bulging eyes. We designed paper-thin powdery wings and splashed them with an array of exquisite colors. Animals will live all over the earth. There will be ones that are creepy crawly, others that fly, some that soar, some will swim, some that are large and in charge and some small and passive.

By early afternoon We began to run out of ideas, so we took a break for lunch. One of Us, I don't remember Who, suggested We take bits and pieces of some of the remarkable creations We had already completed and put them together to fashion new wild life. "BRILLIANT!!" I shouted!! So We took the stripes of the tigers, made them black and white and put them on some horses and called them zebras. We caused some of the mammals to be able to live in the oceans. We took a bird, gave it a long slender neck like a giraffe, long legs like a stork, covered it with beautiful plumes and short stubby wings so it will not be able to fly and called it an ostrich. Some camels had one hump, some had two. Some fish had stripes, some spots; some had lavish fins and tails.

We were having a blast!!

I blessed them saying, "Be fruitful and multiply and fill he waters in the seas and let birds multiply on the earth." (Genesis 1:22.) We made beasts according to its kind and everything that creeps on the earth after its kind. We dropped million and millions of fish and wild life into the seas, a myriad of birds into the sky and watched them swim, fly or crawl off to their pre-established habitation.

We then stood back. We looked up, down and all around. WOW! This was fabulous! *We saw all that We had made, and behold, it was very good.* (Genesis 1:31)

Now for the big finale. Mankind.

We all agreed to create them in Our image. We created them male and female. It would take both forms to fully encompass all the characteristics of God the Father, God the Son and God the Holy Spirit. We created them and then blessed them and told them to be fruitful and multiply. We set them in a splendid garden where We met their every need.

PHEW!! We did all that in six days. Now for a day of rest.

We sat on the front porch on the seventh day and watched it all begin to unfold. I then pronounced that *"It was good, it was very good."*

Now wouldn't you think that this male and female being placed in the pristine setting of a magnificent garden with everything they need to the full of their hearts' content would be able to obey just one simple rule?

One rule and one rule only.

I told them, *"DO NOT EAT FROM THE TREE OF THE KNOWLEDGE OF GOOD AND EVIL."* (Genesis 2:17). I even placed the tree in the middle of the garden so there would not be any confusion as to which tree!

But they did. The serpent, Satan, deceived the woman. *She took from its fruit and ate and she gave it to her husband who was with her and he ate it.* (Genesis 3:6)

Don't get Me wrong. This did not surprise Me. I knew this would happen. I knew that wily serpent would deceive the female and the male would disobey. I did not have to come up with plan B. All of this was My plan A.

Mankind needed a Savior. A Savior who would redeem all of mankind from this original sin of disobedience.

This was the plan. I, God, would leave My heavenly throne and become a man. I will be born of a virgin so that this Savior will be 100% God and 100% man. This Savior would need to be without sin so that He will be worthy to take upon Himself the sin of the whole world and bridge the gap between fallen sinful man and Holy Me.

Confusing, I know. It is the only way. Trust Me. It does take faith.

Faith in Me and faith that this Baby, who will be called Emmanuel, which means God with us, is God in the flesh and will absolve mankind of their sins.

Now to find a virgin girl who will answer the call. I have just the one in mind.

This is where Our story begins.

Or more precisely, where Our story continues.

LUKE 1:26-27 "GOD SENT THE ANGEL GABRIEL TO NAZARETH TO A VIRGIN PLEDGED TO BE MARRIED TO A MAN NAMED JOSEPH."

2

MARY

I remember that it was a particularly warm evening. The sunset had been especially spectacular on the horizon. I love to watch the sunsets through my bedroom window. When my older sister Tamar married and moved out of our house, I was excited to get her bedroom. Now that I am the oldest girl in our home, I get the room with the view. I think I pay for it with the additional chores that have fallen upon me since the departure of Tamar, but it is worth it.

The sunset sent from God was the icing on the cake of the most splendid day. Joseph had come over to the house for dinner with Mama and Abba along with my sister Zipphorah and two little brothers, Amaziah and Levi. I made his favorite meal of roast lamb, sweet potatoes with chopped walnuts and dried figs with honey for dessert. He ate with a hearty appetite. Mama always told me "the best way to a man's heart is through his stomach." We strolled in the warmth of the dusk after dinner and dreamed of our future together. "God, thank You for giving Joseph to me. Help me to be the best possible wife for him." I prayed silently. Mama and Abba are pleased with him also. They have given their blessing to our betrothal.

When Joseph left for the evening we made arrangements for him to come back to our house the next evening after he met with the Rabbi to talk about our wedding ceremony.

God has blessed me more than my wildest imagination. I am so blissfully happy. My skin can hardly contain my exuberance!

Oh, can life get any better than this? "Thank You, God, for giving me abundantly more than I could ask or imagine." This time I said my prayer out loud.

I was humming one of my favorite psalms and preparing for bed. How can I ever fall asleep when my mind is racing with wedding plans

I lay in bed with the cool sheets tucked snuggly around me when a blinding light glowed in the corner of my room. My heart practically jumped out of my chest in fright! My breath left me before I could scream! The light was so brilliantly bright that I could not look at it without it hurting my eyes! I opened my mouth to scream for Abba and that is when I heard a voice coming out of the light that began to take on a human shape-a shape of a man

I froze in utter fear.

"Fear not, Mary," the voice from the glow said to me. *"Rejoice, highly favored one, the LORD is with you. Blessed are you among women."*

I could not begin to comprehend what he was saying.

He continued.

"Do not be afraid Mary, for you have found favor with God."

How did he know my name? I was shaken all the way to my toes.

"Behold, you will conceive in your womb and bring forth a Son, and shall call His name Jesus. He will be great, and will

be called the Son of the Highest and the LORD GOD will give him the throne of His father David. He will reign over the house of Jacob forever, and of His kingdom there shall be no end."

It took several minutes for all this to sink in. A strange calm and peace had by now washed over me and I felt like I had been bathed in the glory of God. Fear was slowly being replaced with tranquility. As the words from what I was now recognizing must be an angel swirled around my head and began to take root, I was struck with the most obvious question.

With a quivering voice I bravely asked the angel, *"But how can this be? Joseph and I are not married yet, and I have been faithful to him. I have not known a man in an intimate way. I have not sinned against God."*

The angel answered, *"The Holy Spirit will come upon you, and the power of the Highest will overshadow you. Therefore, the Holy One that is to be born will be called the Son of God."*

He continued, *"Now let it be known to you that your cousin Elizabeth, has also conceived a son in her old age, and is now in the sixth month for her who was called barren."*

"For nothing is impossible with God.

I sat bolt straight in my bed. Every fiber of my being tingled with a mixture of fear, trepidation and anxiety. Oh my! The list of my emotions could fill this room. The words of the angel kept ringing in my ears. "Highly favored one, the LORD is with you." "Found favor with the LORD. The Holy Spirit will overshadow you."

God had picked out the child's name! Jesus.

But how could this be? The angel even knew about Elizabeth! We had not heard the news of Elizabeth. She and Zachariah must be overjoyed! She carried her barrenness with such shame and disappointment.

What seemed like an eternity since the glory of the Lord had first appeared in my room and awakened me, I was starting to sort out this message from the angel. Well, as much as I could, of course. I still had no idea what all this meant.

This is what I think God was asking me to do.

1. Carry a child from the Holy Spirit.
2. This child will be a boy and he will be called the Son of the Most High.
3. He will rule over the house of Jacob...forever and his kingdom will have no end.

Will that make me a queen mother? Pride began to seep into my heart.

Then a devastating thought gripped my heart! Was this angel, was God asking me to do all this before I marry Joseph? What will he think? How could I expect him to believe such a story? Panic grabbed me at my stomach and worked its icy fingers up to my heart and into my lungs.

NO! Certainly not! God would not ask me to carry such a shameful disgrace.

With that thought, I turned to the shining light that remained in the corner of my room as if he were awaiting my answer with which to swiftly herald back to God.

As the splendid radiance continued to wash over me like a gentle summer rain, my fears seemed to puddle at my feet and evaporate. I gazed into the brilliant light. The icy grip of fear melted away being replaced with an inner sensation I can only describe as miraculous.

Was this the sensation Moses had when God appeared to him in the burning bush? Was this the same sensation Daniel felt when the angel spoke to him and revealed the mystery of the age to come? Am I really counted amongst the greats of my people? He did call me 'favored one' and said 'the LORD is with you.'"

I drew in a deep breath. I had never in my life felt so loved by God! Felt so sure of God's will for my life! I actually started to feel a little giddy inside.

I exhaled the deep breath I realized I had been holding, looked the angel in the eyes and smiled. Bowing my head in reverential awe I said, *"Behold, the handmaid of the LORD. Be it unto me according to your word."*

With that, the angel and the brilliant radiance seemed to turn to leave.

In panic I shouted out, "WAIT!"

He turned in stunned silence.

"May I ask one favor?"

He patiently nodded.

"Can you go tell my Abba what you just told me? I do not want him thinking I have sinned against God".

I think I saw the angel smile with an approving postscript.

And he was gone.

3

Eli

The angel did not have far to go to fulfill the request of Mary. Behind the adjoining wall we lay in seemingly peaceful slumber. We snuggled together under an intricately woven blanket. It was now showing only the slightest of wear by the years of love and children huddled under it against the cold or comforted after a bad dream in the warmth of our arms. Hannah, my wife, and her mother spent months on end weaving it as part of Hannah's dowry. Hannah prayed over every stitch that Jehovah God would bless me and her with many years of love and equal number of children. *Children are a blessing of the Lord, the fruit of the womb is a reward.* (Psalm 127:3)

As Hannah's dreams are filled with pleasantries, I lay next to her in a fitful sleep. How could the council question my loyalty? Who could have brought such false charges against me? Haven't I served the LORD with my whole heart? I have never failed to bring the appropriate sacrifice to the appointed feasts. And surely I am on the line of King David, which should account for something?

The LORD judges His peoples, vindicate me O LORD according to my righteousness and my integrity that is in me. (Psalm 7:8)

As I wrestled with the unexpected turn of events in my life, beneath my closed eyes I saw the glow of a spectacular light. I jumped up out of bed with great alarm! There, in the corner of the room was a bright shining light. So brilliant was it that I had to shield my eyes from its splendor. Terror gripped my heart and my knees began to give way. I lowered myself to the floor and lay prostrate before the glorious glow. I have walked with the LORD long enough to know this to be a vision from God. I have never seen one before, but I have heard stories and read in the Torah of angelic appearances. Fearful, nonetheless, I bowed before the light, which had taken on a human shape.

"Eli," the voice spoke through the light. "Get up, for I am a messenger from the LORD. Do not worship me."

I slowly straightened myself upright and sat cautiously on the side of the bed. As it was still too radiant for me to look directly at the light, I bowed my head and said, "Speak LORD, your servant is listening." I did not know what else to say. What does one say to an apparent visiting angel?

The angel said to me, "Your daughter Mary has found favor with the LORD. She will conceive a child when the Holy Spirit over shadows her. The child within her will be great and shall be called the Son of the Most High. He shall reign over the house of Jacob and His kingdom shall have no end. She is instructed to name the baby Jesus and He will be the Son of God."

The angel stood there for a moment as if to make sure the message had been received. He leaned closer to me to see if I was awake. I sat for several minutes allowing the message to absorb into my weary mind.

"Permit me to speak, O messenger of the LORD. Let me make sure I understand you correctly. God will send the Holy Spirit and miraculously my daughter will be with child without committing any sin? Is this to happen before she marries Joseph?" I quizzically asked the angel.

The angel silently nodded his head.

My daughter will be with child out of wedlock?

The angel interrupted that thought.

He said, "The child will reign and rule and be great. He will be called the Son of the Most High. The Son of God."

I felt tremendous pride begin to swell my heart. My grandson, a king? Then just as suddenly as my swelling heart began to entertain thoughts of grandeur I was reminded of the proverb, 'pride goes before destruction and a haughty spirit before a fall.' (Proverb 16:18). "Forgive me, LORD, for that prideful thought," I quickly prayed. My emotions bounced back and forth like a child's game. One minute I was frozen with fear with what my daughter will be thought of among the community, and the next I was filled with pride that my grandson is destined to rule in the line of King David.

I turned my attention back to the glowing light and the angel.

"So why are you telling me?" I bravely asked the messenger.

"Mary asked me to tell you myself so you would not be displeased with her and think her to be an adulterous woman," replied the messenger.

"What did Mary say to this arrangement?"

The angel genially repeated Mary. "Her words were, 'Behold, the handmaid of the LORD, be it unto me according to your word."

I slowly nodded amiably. "That's my girl!" I said with a wry grin.

As I was entertaining the image in my head of Mary speaking to this angel in the next room, the angel left as suddenly as he had appeared.

I no longer cared what the council thought of me or the actions they threatened to take against me. If God be for me, who can be against me? Right? I stood up, feeling stronger and more energetic than I have in years; I strode the short distance to Mary's room. I was not surprised to find her awake and sitting in bed in stunned bewilderment.

She looked up when I entered the room. Her eyes filled with one enormous query.

"Did you have a visitor tonight, sweetheart?" I asked my precious daughter. With those words, I tenderly laid to rest her overwhelming fears of my disapproval. She leapt into my arms. The foreboding dam that had held back her tears broke into a million little pieces with the strength of my unwavering love and solidarity.

Did God really call my little girl 'favored one'?

MATTHEW 1:18-25 "THE ANGEL OF THE LORD APPEARED TO HIM IN A DREAM AND SAID, 'JOSEPH, SON OF DAVID, DO NOT BE AFRAID TO TAKE MARY HOME AS YOUR WIFE.'"

4

JOSEPH

Man, what a day! Every muscle in my body hurts. I work so hard. Why can't I get ahead? I pray and I pray and I pray but nothing seems to change. Everyone tells me that my carpentry skills are impressive. My father, Jacob, sends me to do the work for his fussiest customers. They always seem pleased with my skills. I do get a few side jobs now and then but it is never steady enough work to make ends meet. Today, Nebat the tanner asked if I wanted to do some apprentice work with him. But to start all over to learn another skill will take time away from my carpentry work.

LORD, what should I do? Please God, send business so I

can work. I am not asking You to send money, I am asking You to send customers so that I can work with the talents with which you have blessed me.

And to top off an already bad day, Mary came to the carpentry shop at my father's house this afternoon. She told me some crazy story that she was with child by the Holy Spirit of God. She said an angel had visited her last night and told her that she was to bear a son and call his name Jesus and he would reign over the house of Jacob forever! Yea, yea, yea. HA! How am I supposed to believe a story like that! Why does she not have the courage, the integrity to tell me the truth!? The truth that she has been unfaithful and that she is not at all the woman I had thought her to be!

I truly love Mary. If she is with child, which I know is not mine, than I love her too much to publicly disgrace her. I am not sure what I can do legally, but I know I cannot marry her now that she has been unfaithful to me.

I am so disappointed!

I am so hurt!

I feel...I feel...so deceived.

I thought she was a good and righteous woman. I don't know what to do from here. I said some horrible things to her and demanded she leave and never show me her face again. I'm not sure I regret making her cry. I am so devastated by her words, her actions. I hardly know what to think.

I set out some cheese and unwrapped some bread for dinner and grabbed a handful of dates. I lay on my cot to rest and regroup. I was too weary to stand any more. My eyelids had grown heavy and I allowed them to close for a few moments.

My thoughts raced around and images flashed behind my closed eyes. I have not been this emotionally drained since Mother's funeral. I no longer cared to eat, and I got up to rewrap the food. I put the cheese away and prepared for bed. Lying on my cot, I tried once again to sort out the day. Exhaustion won the tug of war with my conscience, and I finally fell asleep. I have no idea how long I had been lying there when I heard a voice.

I saw through my closed eyes a glow, which began to rise behind me. Startled and fearful that it was a fire, I frantically searched for a blanket to smother the flames! As

I turned, I was more frightened by what I saw than had it been a fire! I shielded my face from the intense radiance of the glow that was beginning to fill my small home.

"Joseph, Son of David, do not be afraid to take Mary as your wife," said a voice coming from the light. *"For that which is conceived in her is of the Holy Spirit. She will bring forth a Son, and you shall call His name Jesus, for He will save His people from their sins."*

To say the least, I was dumbstruck! OH MY GOODNESS! Mary was telling me the truth! A son? Named Jesus? He shall save His people from their sins? What did that mean? I had read in the Torah of angelic visitors but never dreamed in a million years that one would visit me.

I needed some clarification.

"May I ask you a question?"

The angel seemed to nod yes.

"So Mary was telling me the truth?"

Again the angel nodded affirmation.

"So she is with child?"

Again, and without agitation, the angel nodded

attesting to the truth.

"By the Holy Spirit of God?"

Another nod with a slight smile that the message was beginning to sink in.

"His name is to be Jesus? He will save His people, the Jews, from their sins?"

Now the angel kept nodding as the questions kept coming.

"I am to be His father? I am to be the father of the Son of God? Will you be there to help us?"

"God will be with you," the angel said with delight and unwavering assurance.

I relished this tranquil state of sleep for several moments. I had never felt so at peace with God. So loved by Him. So much in the center of His will for my life. My future wife and mine.

In my dream state, I looked at the angel who seemed to be awaiting some sort of response from me. I knew what my answer would be. What my answer must be.

"Yes." I boldly told the angel. Almost shouting it. "I will not be afraid to take Mary as my wife. I will do the very best job I know to be a good husband and the father to...to...to whom? The Son of God?"

Oh my goodness! I thought. How does one go about fathering the Son of the Most High?

And with my final words, the angel left as quickly as he had come.

I opened my eyes. Had I dozed off? I was completely disoriented. I sat up shaking my head, trying to distinguish reality from dream. Was that a dream I just had? It seemed so real. I was sure that God had spoken to me in my sleep.

Mary? The mother of God's Son? How could this be? Why her? Why us? She will be with child and we are not married. What will the town's people think? What will my father think?

"God," I prayed, "Thank You for choosing us to do your bidding. I am overwhelmed that you find me worthy enough to raise Your Son. Truthfully God, I am scared to death. *You are my strength and shield and my heart trusts in You.* (Psalm 28:7) You have always been a very faithful God."

As those consoling words soothed me like a warm fire on a cold night, I sunk deeper and deeper into my cot and felt those stirring words from the angel clear away all my fear and doubt.

The anguish on Mary's face would not leave my mind. The images of her begging me to believe her were fused behind my eyes and branded into my heart. I replayed the scene in my head of her pleading with me to listen her. I said some really harsh things to her. I wince at my own words toward her. I had to go to Mary and ask her to forgive me for being so belligerent towards her

Fortunately I had fallen asleep in my clothes; so after washing up and without anything to eat, I ran to Mary's house, not really caring if it was too early. I knew Mary had much responsibility in her home and that she usually rises early in order to get them all completed.

Had Mary told her parents? She did not have time to tell

me when she had come to the shop yesterday to bring me the news. I hastily jumped to conclusions and said some regrettable things to her that made her cry and run off before she could speak any further.

How will we tell her parents? "LORD GOD, HELP! Please go before me and prepare their hearts to receive this news. Give me the right words to speak to them. Help me accept whatever emotions they will have."

I reached Mary's house just as the townspeople were waking up and moving about to begin another day. My heart soared as I saw her outside hanging the day's laundry on the clothesline on top of their roof.

"MARY!" I yelled, probably too loudly.

"Mary!" Reaching her I hardly knew where to begin.

She looked down on me from her place on duty on the roof. Even from this distance I could tell her eyes were swollen and red from hours of crying. I would not blame her if she refused to see me and hear my words of explanation.

"Mary," I said for the third time. I walked up the side

staircase to join her on the roof. She did not acknowledge my presence and continued with her work. "Mary, please forgive me for my rude and harsh words yesterday. I did not believe your story. But last night an angel appeared to me too and told me not to be afraid to take you as my wife. He told me everything! Oh Mary! I cannot believe that God has chosen us to be the parents of His Son. What an awesome and daunting task with which He has entrusted us."

Mary stood there shocked and I'm sure a bit embarrassed by my exuberance. But I did not care. I loved her and was so ashamed of my action the day before that I needed desperately to hear Mary's words of forgiveness.

I could tell that Mary did not want to look at me. She continued to hang the clothes as I gushed my apology. After she hung the last shirt she turned to me. I was filled with shame that I had caused her so much obvious pain. She looked wounded, scorned, maligned. I wanted to hug her and comfort her, but I knew I could not do that in public.

I tried to hug her with my words. "Mary, I love you. I will never, ever make you cry again. Please forgive me. I was so mortified by your words, I was only thinking of myself and not of you."

"Oh Joseph," she slowly began, her voice dotted with staccato notes and full of foreboding. "What are we going to do? I am so scared." She managed to sputter out in between sobs. Mary looked around and throwing caution to the wind, stepped toward me and laid her head on my chest. She exhaled her pent up anxiety and unashamedly let her tears of exhaustion and fear soak my shirt. I wrapped my arms around her and we stood in silence until I felt her body begin to relax.

I said to her in reassurance, "The angel said that God will be with us. "He will instruct thee and teach thee the way which you should go. I will guide thee with my eyes." (Psalm 32:8)Everything will be all right. If God is with us who can be against us?

LUKE 1:5-23 & 2:57-80 "DO NOT BE AFRAID, ZECHARIAH, YOUR PRAYER HAS BEEN HEARD. YOUR WIFE ELIZABETH WILL BEAR YOU A SON AND YOU ARE TO GIVE HIM THE NAME JOHN."

5

ZECHARIAH

So there I was doing my priestly duty. Thank God, King Herod of Judea allowed us to continue to worship the LORD. I am from the line of Aaron, which makes me eligible to enter the temple to give the appropriate sacrifice. My wife, Elizabeth is from the line of Aaron also. We have lived a righteous life. We have always been careful to observe the laws of the LORD. That is why she and I are both so perplexed, so disheartened that the LORD has not blessed us with children. Elizabeth's barrenness has been the cause of much shame and ridicule from the people. They silently think there must be sin in her life for her to suffer this perceived judgment from God. I must admit, I have thought that of other barren women. Surely they must have a hidden sin for God to withhold such a tremendous blessing upon them. Funny how things change when the sandal is on the other foot.

But with Elizabeth I know differently. She has been my partner, my soul mate. We have loved each other since we were children and we were very happy when our parents arranged for our marriage. We presumed we would have several children. *"Children are a blessing from God. Blessed is the man whose quiver is full."* (Psalm 127:3 &5). Wasn't that a promise from God? Am I not blessed by God then? Have I somehow not found favor in His eyes for Him to withhold this precious blessing from Elizabeth and me?

I have wrestled with this thought for fifty years now. Elizabeth and I just celebrated fifty years of marriage. Yes, the years have been full and happy with the joy and laughter of children that belong to our family and friends. But it is not the same. Elizabeth smiles, but the smile does not reach her eyes. She has been a wonderful wife. She has served the LORD with me faithfully for fifty years. In our old age, we have become resigned to the fact that we will never be parents. I try to hide my disappointment from Elizabeth. She carries the blame of her barrenness. Yes, she has lots of friends but some of the women speak cruel words behind her back. They pass judgment on her as if they are God. It is maddening at times.

These were the thoughts running through my head as I headed into the temple to burn the incense. Our division of priests were on duty that week and I was chosen by lot, as is the custom. When the time for the burning of incense came, all the assembled worshipers were praying outside. I was in the sanctuary when an angel of the LORD appeared, standing to the right of the incense altar. I was overwhelmed with fear!! But the angel said, *"Don't be afraid, Zechariah! For God has heard your prayer and your wife, Elizabeth, will bear you a son! And you are to name him John. You will have great joy and gladness and many will rejoice with you at his birth. For he will be great in the eyes of the LORD. He must never touch wine or hard liquor and he will be filled with the Holy Spirit even before his birth. And he will persuade many Israelites to turn to the LORD their God. He will be a man with the spirit and power of Elijah, the prophet of old. He will precede the coming of the LORD, preparing the people for His arrival. He will turn the hearts of the fathers to their children, and he will change disobedient minds to accept godly wisdom."*

I said to the angel, *"How can I know this will happen? I am an old man now, and my wife is also well along in years."*

Then the angel said, *"I am Gabriel! I stand in the very presence of God. It was He who sent me to bring you this good news! And now, since you did not believe what I said, you won't be able to speak until the child is born. For my words will certainly come true at the proper time."*

I stood there like a fool with my mouth hanging open. Good thing no one was around to see my foolishness. I could not believe what I just heard! Elizabeth will be with child in her old age! HA! What will the people call her, Sarah!

Gabriel? Is that what the angel said his name was? Wasn't that the name of the angel that appeared to Daniel? Naw, it couldn't be? Could it? His clothes were so striking and extraordinary and remarkable!

What did Gabriel say about the baby? OH! I can't remember it all! Think man, think. I pounded my head with the palm of my hand as if that would jog my memory. He said...he said... "He would be great in the eyes of the LORD, he must not drink wine or hard drink. He will be filled with the Holy Spirit and have the spirit and power of Elijah.' What does that mean? He will prepare the arrival of the Lord.

And what were his parting words? I will not be able to speak until the child is born because of my unbelief?

I opened my mouth to test the angel. I started to recite the shama. "Hear O Israel, the LORD is God." Nothing came out. I could hear the words in my head but no audible sound came out of my mouth. Oye vay. What has just happened to me?

I have no idea how long I was in the sanctuary. But I had a feeling it was longer than routine. The people outside must be getting worried. When I finally did come out, I could not speak to them.

The crowd gathered around me. They wanted to know what had taken so long and what had happened in the temple. I opened my mouth to speak but nothing came out. Not even a squeak. I stayed for the remainder of my service and then went home to Elizabeth.

She was not going to believe what just happened.

LUKE 1:39-56 "AT THAT TIME MARY GOT READY AND HURRIED TO A TOWN IN THE HILL COUNTRY OF JUDEA, WHERE SHE ENTERED ZECHARIAH'S HOME AND GREETED ELIZABETH."

6

ELIZABETH

I still laugh when I think about that day! Zechariah had been at the temple all week. He would be coming home that evening. I was preparing his favorite meal. My cousin, Hannah always said, "The way to a man's heart is through his stomach." Very true words, I thought to myself and chuckled. Zechariah was an enthusiastic eater. It always warmed my heart to watch him enjoy my cooking. It made all the labor of food preparation worth it. It never quite eased the pain of setting a table for two and not ten. But those days of barrenness are over! How kind is the Lord. He has taken away my disgrace of having no children!

I could hardly believe I was in my sixth month already. Zechariah and I had been in seclusion since the day he came home from the temple and could not speak. I have to admit at first it was kind of amusing to have him pantomime or write down everything he wanted to say. After a while it became wearisome to him and he would sit in silence. However, it did give him more time to read and study the Torah. Friends and family came to visit at the beginning. I think they came out of morbid curiosity than of a show of comfort and support. I guess I don't blame them. It was a novelty. A grown man who could not utter a word or a sound. Nothing came out of his mouth. Nothing, nada, dabar.

We had received word that my cousin Mary was hoping to visit us soon. I was puzzled by a dream I had a few days ago. I think it was a message from God. I think God was telling me that Mary was the fulfillment of the scripture in Isaiah, *'All right then, the Lord Himself will choose the sign. Look! The virgin will conceive a child! She will give birth to a son and will call him Immanuel--'God is with us."* (Isaiah 7:14)

Could Mary be the chosen virgin? She has not married Joseph yet.

It was not a very far journey from Hannah and Eli's home in Galilee to our house in the hill country of Judea. I don't know when to expect her. But I couldn't go anywhere in my condition, so I waited for her to show up at any time. At least I knew we would be home and not have her waiting for our return. One day I was cleaning up the dinner dishes when I heard footsteps at our door.

"Elizabeth? Zechariah? Are you home?" I heard the familiar young voice.

When I heard Mary's greeting the baby leapt in my womb! It was the oddest sensation! Not having experienced carrying a child before, I had no references but this was the most awe-inspiring sensation and I felt as if I was filled with the Holy Spirit myself! I opened the door to see my dear sweet cousin Mary.

As if God was speaking through me, in a loud voice I said to her, *"You are blessed by God above all other women, and your child is blessed. What an honor this is that the mother of my Lord should visit me! As soon as the sound of your greeting reached my ears, the baby in my womb leaped for joy. You are blessed because you believed that the Lord would do what He said." (Luke 1:42-45)*

Mary looked at me in stunned silence. Wide eyed she asked, "How did you know I was with child?

I'll never forget what she said next.

"Oh how I praise the Lord. How I rejoice in God my Savior! For He took

notice of His lowly servant girl and now generation after generation will call me blessed for the Mighty One has done great things for me. His mercy extends to those who fear Him from generation to generation. He has performed mighty deeds with His arm; He has scattered those who are proud in their inmost thoughts. He has brought down rulers from their thrones but has lifted up the humble. He has filled the hungry with good things but has sent the rich away empty. He has helped His servant Israel remembering to be merciful to Abraham and his descendants forever even as He said to our fathers." (Luke 1:46-55)

My eyes overflowed with tears of joy with her words of adoration to our God. Surely the Lord is gracious and merciful. My dream was indeed a message from God. Mary is the fulfillment of the scripture. Mary is the chosen vessel of God. He certainly knew that He picked the right one. Mary is a devout worshiper of Jehovah. She will be a great mother to God's Son. She has just enough spunk to carry this load.

Mary stayed with us until my baby was born.

As I perceived that time for the baby was drawing near, together we made preparations. Zechariah had a small crib built to set beside our bed. Hannah had sent many of her baby items she had been keeping. Mary said her mother stayed up for three nights embroidering on the blanket. It was very precious to me. The whole town seemed to have been celebrating with anticipation the birth of our son. Funny that we know it is a boy. God even told us his name. John. That is not a family name. I wonder why God chose it.

It was the day after the Sabbath when I felt the first birth pangs. Mary was so calm for her young age. I know she was watching me and how much pain I was experiencing, knowing that she would be in the same predicament in a few short months. Mary ran to get Abijah, the midwife, who had come to visit me a few days ago and agreed that the baby would be here soon.

Abijah took control. She brought clean cloths and instructed Mary to draw some water and keep it warm. Zechariah had left the house to go wherever it is men go when their wives are giving birth. This was no place for a man to be anyway.

God was very gracious to this old woman and the labor and delivery went as smoothly as possible. As the sun was setting and the room was growing dark, Mary had lit a low burning lamp that cast a warm welcoming light. With my last ounce of strength I gave birth to a healthy baby boy; a boy who would grow to be the forerunner of the Christ. Abijah had instructed Mary to pour the warmed water into the basin and pour the vial of fragrant oil she had pulled out of her apron pocket.

Abijah wrapped the pink crying baby in a new white cloth and began to wash him with the scented warm water. She was so gentle and loving to John. She spoke as she worked, "Oh don't cry, sweetie pie. I'm here to make things all better for you. Now, now. What is all this fuss about? I'm doing the best I can. Shhhh little baby, I'll get you to your mama in just a minute." She cut and tied the umbilical cord, dabbed the blood with a different cloth and swattled John in Hannah's newly embroidered blanket. She gently placed John in my arms. I have never been so filled with joy! I let the tears stream down my face unabashedly. Mary too was overcome with joy and shared my tears. I could read in her face that she was anticipating her own delivery.

Abijah had a second basin of fresh warm water and a different vial of scented oil. She placed a small cloth in the basin and began to bathe me. She began to wash away the perspiration from my brow and my neck. It was the most beautiful pampering I had ever received. In my euphoric state, I relinquished John into the waiting arms of Mary and allowed Abijah to minister to me. I closed my eyes, so exhausted, so exhilarated, so at peace, so in love with my God.

I must have fallen asleep because when I opened my eyes, Abijah had cleaned up and gone home and Mary was slicing some bread and fruit. Zechariah was sitting in the chair by the fire, holding John. He was speaking to him but no words came out. I could see John's little eyes staring at his big ol' Abba! Could he understand the old man without words? Zechariah too had long awaited this birth. Thank you God that it all went well, I prayed silently. With the scene of Zechariah and John dancing in my head, all the years of shame and disgrace of being barren faded away like morning fog being chased by the rising of the warm morning sun.

On the eighth day the priests came to circumcise John. They insisted that we should name the baby after Zechariah but I spoke up and said, 'NO! He is to be called John." They said to me, "There is no one among your relatives who has that name." Then they made signs to Zechariah to find our what he would like to name the child. He asked for a writing tablet and to everyone's astonishment he wrote, 'His name is John.' Immediately his mouth was opened and his tongue was loosed and he began to speak praising God. The neighbors were all filled with awe and through out the hill country of Judea people were talking about all these things. Everyone who heard this wondered about it, asking, 'What then is this child going to be?' For the Lord's hand was with him." (Luke 1:59-66)

"Zechariah was filled with the Holy Spirit and he stood among the people and prophesied, "Praise be to the LORD, the God of Israel, because He has come and has redeemed His people. He has raised up a horn of salvation for us in the house of his servant David as He said

through His holy prophets of long ago, salvation from our enemies and from the hand of all who hate us- to show mercy to our fathers and to remember His holy covenant, the oath He swore to our father Abraham, to rescue us from the hand of our enemies and to enable us to serve Him without fear in holiness and righteousness before Him all our days."

"And you, my child, will be called prophet of the Most High; for you will go on before the Lord to prepare the way for Him, to give His people the knowledge of salvation through the forgiveness of their sins, because of the tender mercy of our God by which the rising sun will come to us from heaven to shine on those living in darkness and in the shadow of death, to guide our feet into the path of peace."(Luke 1:67-79)

And John grew and became strong in spirit and he lived in the desert until he appeared publicly to Israel. (Luke 1:80)

LUKE 1:59 "MARY STAYED WITH ELIZABETH FOR ABOUT THREE MONTHS AND THEN RETURNED HOME."

7

MARY

I stayed with Zechariah and Elizabeth for a few more weeks. The women of the town were so ecstatic and excited for them that it was apparent she would be in no short supply of help. Every day someone came to visit and brought food and gifts. Elizabeth was exhausted by day's end just from smiling and laughing so much. It was as if the whole town was bursting at the seams with elation for her and Zechariah. Even the men came by to pat Zechariah on the back and give their congratulations.

I packed up my few belongings and prepared to depart after breakfast. Elizabeth had bundled up John and even

Zechariah joined us as they walked me partly on my journey. I could tell Elizabeth was regaining her strength. Her gait was strong and purposeful. She carried John as if he weighed nothing at all.

We stopped at the group of sycamore trees to say our final farewells. We did not live too far apart and knew that we would see each other again soon. Still it was a bittersweet departure. The three of them huddled together like a cluster of grapes as I joined the group of fellow travelers and began to walk towards Nazareth. My heart was so full of joy and my head was so filled with pleasant memories of the past three months.

I was by now beginning to feel the baby move in my body. At first I thought I had eaten something disagreeable with me. My stomach churned and gurgled. When I mentioned it to Elizabeth, she smiled the knowing smile of a special, well-kept secret. "It must be Jesus turning over to kneel in prayer." She joked with a sparkle in her eyes.

After the reassurance that I was not ill, I relished the moments in which I felt the baby stir. With each passing week I began to feel Him almost daily. If I sat in a chair or lay in my bed very still I could see my stomach move and change shape. It was so very thrilling and I could not wait to get back to Joseph and share this with him. Will he be as elated as I? Will he consider this to be his baby too even though we know it is not? God did call him to play a very significant role in this...in this...plan of salvation.

As the sun grew hot I was relieved to see Galilee come in to view. I was almost home! I wanted to run but knew I was not a little girl any more and needed to remind myself that I was now a young lady, a betrothed young lady and betrothed young ladies do not run. But I felt as capricious as a child with a new toy anxious to take it outside to play. I did permit myself to skip a bit when I was not passing by people.

I do not know why I thought Galilee should look different. But it was the same as it had always been. Everything in this small town was just as I had left it three months ago. Nothing ever changes here. No good thing ever comes out of Galilee.

My brothers and sister saw me walking towards the house long before I saw them. They came running out to greet me. They were excited to see me and like a big noisy parade we all marched home as if I was a long lost prodigal returning from a distant land. It sure was good to be home. Mama had the table prepared for a welcome home meal. She insisted I sit and be waited on..."one last time", she said to me with a wink. The special treatment will last for the rest of the day, for tomorrow I would resume my usual round of chores. The thought of my old routine actually brought a bit of relief for I longed to regain some normalcy back to my life.

The children instantly started talking over top of each other about the events that had taken place in my absence.

"Jesse's cow fell in the creek and six men had to hoist her out. They used four new ropes and it took them most of the day! The whole town went down to watch," shouted the youngest, Levi, the animal lover.

"Leah and Salome were arguing at the well...again" Zipporah, my youngest sister, breathlessly announced, "and Leah threw Salome's bucket down the well and they started a big argument and their husbands had to come and drag them home. You should have seen those two big ol' ladies tugging at each other's scarves and throwing dirt. It was funny!"

I glanced at Mama sideways. She just raised her eyebrows and rolled her eyes. I knew those two women have been at odds since Leah and Saul, her husband, refused Salome's son as a husband for their daughter.

"And the biggest news of all!" butted in Amaziah, my brother closest in age to me, "Abinadab's barn caught fire!! Abba and I and the whole town ran to try and help dowse the flames! Abba and Asa ran into the burning barn to get the animals out. Several other men formed a line and handed buckets of water back and forth from the well! It was a huge fire!!"

I looked at Abba who was slowly shaking his head as his memory filled with that horrible night. I noticed his hands had been bandaged but had not had a chance to ask why.

"It was a total loss," he finally said gravely.

The room fell silent as the retelling of the tragedy replayed in their minds.

"Are Abinadab and Josephine and the family okay?" I asked.

"Yes. Thank God and after the Sabbath we will all help rebuild," Abba reported with strong conviction.

I let the grief wash over the room for a moment.

"I got to hold Elizabeth's baby" I tried to break the sadness with some news of joy.

Their eyes looked up at mine with excitement, and the mourning spell seemed to have been broken.

I recounted all the events that took place in my world while in Judea. How Zachariah had gone mute until the baby was named. That was wild. I had never seen nor heard of anything like that before. I recalled stories of how Zachariah would try to communicate and then eventually he became too exhausting and frustrating and he passed the days in silence. Elizabeth was so overjoyed to finally start a family. God had renewed her strength for her age. *'Those who wait upon the LORD shall be renewed with strength,'* the scripture from Isaiah, ran through my mind. I marveled as I watched her endure the labor and then regain her energy after John was born. He sure gained weight by the time I left their home. He will be a big strapping boy.

I wasn't sure how much my siblings knew about the baby that I was carrying. Did Mama and Abba tell them about the angelic visit? I will have to ask them the first chance I get.

After dinner dishes were washed, there was still enough daylight left for me to go and visit Joseph. He was so glad to see me! We took a brief stroll among the grove of trees as I told him all about my visit with Zachariah and Elizabeth. He was shocked to hear that an angel too had visited them and that Zechariah had lost his voice because he did not believe what the angel was telling him. I told him how Zechariah had to use a writing tablet to write down the name John when they took John to be circumcised. Then his tongue was loosed and he could speak. I told him that watching Elizabeth deliver John gave me great strength that I can endure when it comes to my turn.

I spoke as fast as I could because I knew it was getting dark. He kissed me on the top of my head and gave me a welcome home hug. In my haste I had forgotten to tell him about the baby moving. I'll tell him when I see him tomorrow.

What do the next few months have in store for me?

8

JOSEPH

I think back on the betrothal party often. Mary looked as beautiful as I had ever seen her. She had pinned honeysuckle flowers in her hair under her scarf. I could smell them all through the room. The tables had been decorated with honeysuckle vines and blossoms. Everyone seemed so happy for us. They seemed to have known this day would come eventually. Although our parents had their hand in our marriage arrangements, it seems Eli had me picked out for Mary shortly after her birth! He is a very wise man. He loves his daughters very much.

That is why my dowry had to be very special. I knew I would make something extraordinary to show how much I love and value Mary. My friend, Kish, suggested I make a cedar chest with intricate carvings depicting scenes of Nazareth in the four seasons. Father helped me find the finest wood and even helped me in the construction. He has incredible skills. That wood is like putty in his hands. He seemed to be able to make it do whatever he wanted it to do. Father even let me use his favorite carving tools to engrave each scene around the box.

I finished the box and waxed it down with deer hide oil I purchased from Nebal. I put on four coats of the oil just like he suggested. After each coat dried, I buffed and polished the box and then applied the next coat. This process took an entire week! But the end results were amazing. You could almost see your reflection in the high polished wood. The cedar chest was nearly as beautiful as Mary.

Not only did I have the dowry to make but also I had to build onto my father's house to prepare a home for us. Again, my father helped me a great deal. I was working on the finish touches the day Mary came to tell me of her visits from the angel. I had been working on the kitchen that particular day so Mary was very much on my mind. As I made shelves and cooking areas for her I dreamed of all the meals she would prepare for our future children and me. I practically daydreamed the day away. Several times Father nudged me out of my fantasy to get me back to work. He smiled and gave me a hard time in a good-natured way. He knew what I was thinking. He had loved Mother very much. I think Mary reminded him a bit of her. Maybe that is why he liked her so much. Mother's death had been hard on him. Half of him died with her. They truly were one flesh. I can only hope my marriage is as happy as theirs. I know I will do everything in my power with God's help to make a wonderful home for Mary and our children. The first child will be here before I know it.

I still cannot believe that Mary and I have been chosen to raise the Son of God! Who am I to receive such a calling, such a blessing? I sure hope Mary was taught well how to care for a baby because I haven't a clue what to do. My hands are so rough I'll probably scratch the little guy. He will certainly be able to tell who is holding him just by the feel of our hands!

A son! I'm going to have a son! I would find myself daydreaming about Him too. It's a wonder I got any work done! As I was building our home and putting the stones in place for the fireplace I fantasized about playing with Him. I will build Him some toys and teach Him the trade. I will do just as my father had done. He had started me off with sanding the wood. That is the most critical part of carpentry work. I got my first carving knife at age eight and by ten I was very adept with the saws. I will teach Him everything I know.

I can't wait!!

But first things first.

We would have to wait until after the baby was born to officially get married. I had my two witnesses at the ready. My two best buddies, Kish and Eliab. We had known each other all our lives. Boy, did we have some fun together. Some of it our parents never heard about, if you know what I mean! We played hacky sack all the time. We pestered our mothers to sew the cloth ball and we filled them with sand. We hiked to the neighboring towns and spied on the young girls as they came to the well each morning to draw water. Kish was sure he would marry one of them but there was no way we would marry outside of our faith. Eliab's father was a high priest. His escapades kept his father on his knees. I don't think he ever lived up to his father's expectations. Maybe that is why he was such a daredevil. Always seeing how close to the edge he could get with out getting caught. I guess negative attention is better than none at all.

Kish, on the other hand always played it safe. He was our look out guy. Eliab would think of something daring to do, I would strategize to see if it was feasible and Kish would watch to make sure the coast was clear and no one was coming. Some of the town's people called us hellions. Ha! They just don't know how to have fun! Well we had enough fun for all of them. Most of it was good clean fun. So we broke a few things along the way and had to work to pay it off or clean it up.

More than once I heard my father say in exasperation, "Why can't you be more like your bother Jotham?"

"Because he doesn't have an adventurous bone in his body,

Dad." I would respond in a smart mouth reply. A swift cuff to the back of my head usually followed that statement. Father was not amused. Not that I was disobedient to him or Mother. I really tried to be obedient, I just thought there was a big world out there and I wanted to see what it had to offer. Eliab seemed to be out for revenge. He was born with a chip on his shoulder and every chance he got he tried to knock it off. He is married now with three boys of his own. I bet one of them is his father's payback.

It is not surprising that Kish continued with his education and is a scribe working with the priests. He always took learning the Torah very seriously. I wonder why God did not choose him to be the father to His Son? Kish always seemed more righteous than I. But who know the mind of God?

As is the custom of the Hebrews, the bride awaits her bridegroom and does not know when he will come for her. So when it is time for the actual wedding day, Kish and Eliab have talked me into coming for Mary in the middle of the night. If I know Mary, she'll be expecting just that. She knows Kish and Eliab all too well. She smiles at Kish and prays for Eliab.

So that is the game plan. I can hardly wait!

LUKE 2:1-3 "IN THOSE DAYS CAESAR AUGUSTUS ISSUED A DECREE THAT A CENSUS SHOULD BE TAKEN OF THE ENTIRE ROMAN WORLD."

9

CAESAR AUGUSTUS

I walked around the palace grounds marveling at the beauty of it all. The good times make one forget the bad times and the bad times make one wonder if life is worth living. I am currently living in the former. Rome has been charting a course of smooth sailing for many years now. At the meeting of the senate yesterday they gave me a report of the state of affairs of the empire.

The people were starting to call it Pax Romana, Roman peace. We had added much land to the empire. The senate said Rome was the greatest empire ever built.

And all the credit is due to me! I established a road system. I established a waterway in which water flows freely to the people in aqua ducts and there is no need to go to communal water wells like the savages in the east. My army is the finest ever to be trained. Their iron shields and swords are made with the most superior iron ore in the land. They are swift in foot and dexterous with sword. Their hearts are that of lions and their loyalty to Rome is its equal.

I have established a policing force to ensure order and protection of the citizens. I have developed a trained company of men that will assist this policing force and defend against fire and damage control. I have created a courier system to quickly and securely send messages around my entire empire.

I and I alone have done this.

Although the senate thinks Rome to be a republic, I rule with autonomy. I am Caesar. My word is law. The senate knows if they defy me that my loyal army will effectively persuade them into compliance or forcefully remove them from their position of over-inflated sense of self-aggrandizement. Over-stuffed buffoons, that is what they are. They walk through the streets as if they have anything to do with the structure and affluence of the empire and its citizens.

I loathe the lot of them.

They all objected when I announced I would decree a census across the empire. In fact, I sent the couriers out yesterday morning before the congress convened. As if they can tell me what I can and cannot do! The gall of them! There have been censuses before but no one thought to have the people travel to their place of birth to be registered! Think of the revenue for all that traveling! The taxes alone just for the journey will be enormous! I even amaze myself at times with my sheer genius.

After I announced my decision to register the people according to their birthplace, the senate erupted into debate. They tried to tell me I was unreasonable, that the people would rebel and their loyalty to Rome would wane. They thought the Roman citizens would believe that this census would give equal right to the barbarians of the rest of the empire.

I, of course, have already thought of that and stated in the decree that the census was for numbering and taxation only. I emphatically stated that this census would in no way grant any rights, privileges or access to the civil liberties of those of natural born Romans.

The fools! I know what is best for my people. I know how the Roman citizens think and what they want. They love Rome as much as I do. They want to keep the Roman race pure and free from outside contamination. The gods love Rome and Rome loves her gods.

I dispatched 1500 couriers to all parts of the empire. They were instructed to enter every city, town and village to post the decree. They were to take the summons to the ruler whom I had installed and hand deliver it directly to them. I would accept no excuse for a providence not to be in compliance with my decree. The couriers were to return to me no later than the second full moon.

With the glory and power of total domination coursing through my veins, I reclined on a chaise lounge chair on the palace terrace overlooking the splendor of Rome. Basking in the sun I could feel the gods smiling down upon me. I could feel their strength in me.

I am a god.

10

JOSEPH

I will be the first to admit that I am not a very educated man. I know that I am from the tribe of Judah, in the lineage of King David. Oh to have some of his wealth right now. That sure would make things easier. I go to temple; I make my sacrifices and yearly offerings. I listen to the rabbis, but I am not well versed in the Torah.

I remember hearing a rabbi speak on Sabbath in the temple about God foretelling of His 'Chosen One, His Messiah.' I remember being puzzled when the rabbi read from Isaiah that a *virgin shall be with child and shall bear a son and His name shall be called Emmanuel.'* (Isaiah 7:14) Is that virgin

Mary? Was Isaiah speaking of my Mary?

I went to see Mary's cousin, Zechariah, in the hill country of Judea. I did not know whom else to trust. I knew he knew of Mary's baby and the visit from the angel. Surely he would help me search the scriptures to see what God had told us about this virgin birth.

I found out that God did not say much. We found that the prophet Micah had said, *"Now gather yourselves in troops, O daughter of troops. They have laid siege against us; with a rod they will smite the judge of Israel with a rod on the cheek. But as for you, Bethlehem Ephrathah, too little to be among the clans of Judah, from you One will go forth from Me to be ruler in Israel. His goings forth are from long ago, from the days of eternity. Therefore, He will give them up until the time when she who is in labor has borne a child. Then the remainder of His brethren will return to the sons of Israel. And He will arise and shepherd His flock in the strength of the LORD, in the majesty of the name of the LORD His God. And they will remain because at the time He will be great to the ends of the earth. And this One will be our peace."* Micah 5:1-5

Zechariah had explained to me that this is indicating that the Christ was prophesied to be born in Bethlehem Ephrathah.

"In the city of David?" I marveled out loud. "In the city of my ancestors?"

Zechariah then took me in the scripture to the prophet Isaiah again. The king of Judah at the time that Isaiah lived was Ahaz. He was frightened because two kings, Rezin, king of Syria and Pekah, the son of Remalilah, the king of Israel, were coming up to Jerusalem to wage war against it. God told Isaiah to go to King Ahaz to reassure him that God will protect Jerusalem.

"Then God did the strangest thing." Zechariah added his commentary. "Ahaz must not have believed Isaiah, so God instructed Isaiah to tell Ahaz to *'ask a sign for yourself from the LORD your God; make it deep as Sheol or high as heaven. But Ahaz said 'I shall not ask, not will I test the LORD?"* *Then Isaiah said, "Listen now, O house of David! Is it too slight a thing for you to try the patience of men, that you will try the patience of my God as well? Therefore the LORD Himself will give you a sign; Behold, a virgin will be with child and bear a son, and she will call His name Emmanuel. He will eat curds and honey at the time He knows enough to refuse evil and choose good.'"* (Isaiah 7:13-16)

I asked Zechariah, "The virgin birth is a sign? A sign of what? A sign telling us what?"

Then Zechariah pointed out more scripture in Isaiah. He thought this too pointed to the Christ.

"People who walk in darkness will see a great light; those who live in a dark land, the light will shine on them. Thou shalt multiply the nation, thou shalt increase their gladness;

they will be glad in Thy presence as with the gladness of harvest, as men rejoice when they divide the spoil. For Thou shalt break the yoke of their burden and the staff on their shoulders, the rod of their oppressor, as at the battle of Midian. For every boot of the booted warrior in the battle tumult and cloak filled in blood, will be for burning, fuel for the fire. For a child will be born to us, a son will be given to us, and the government will rest on His should and His name will be called Wonderful Counselor, Mighty God, Eternal Father, Prince of Peace. There will be no end to the increase of His government or of peace, on the throne of David and over His kingdom, to establish it and to uphold it with justice and righteousness from then on and forevermore. The zeal of the LORD of hosts will accomplish this." (Isaiah 9:2-7)

I mused on this for a while. This baby, Jesus, will shine a light in the darkness, multiply nations and increase their gladness? He will break the yoke of their oppressor and there will not be need for an army? He will be called Wonderful Counselor, Mighty God...Prince of Peace? He will sit on the throne of David and His kingdom will never end?

WOW! I am supposed to be the father to this future king? This Mighty God?

If God has foretold that His Christ will be born in Bethlehem Ephrathah, how am I supposed to get Mary to Bethlehem?

Zechariah was looking at me as my mind was racing. Our eyes met. He had a disturbing look on his face.

He said slowly and soberly, "Now Joseph, before you get too excited about raising the next king of Israel, there is one more passage about which you should know. I am not sure what it all means; I am not sure what a lot of this means. This passage is not so bright and glorious. It is downright distressing and very ominous. Actually I am not sure you even want to hear it. God makes it sound like this Son of His; this Son of yours has a tough road ahead of Him. I just trust and have confidence that God has a mighty plan for His people." It says further in Isaiah.

'Who has believed our message? And to whom has the arm of the LORD been revealed? For He grew up before Him like a tender shoot, and like a root out of the parched ground; He has no stately form or majesty that we should look upon Him, nor appearance that we should be attracted to Him. He was despised and forsaken of men, a man of sorrows and acquainted with grief; and like one from whom men hide their face. He was despised and we did not esteem Him. Surely our grief's He Himself bore, and our sorrows He carried. Yet we ourselves esteemed Him stricken, smitten of God and afflicted. But He was pierced through for our transgressions, He was crushed for our iniquities; the chastening of our well being fell upon Him and by His scourging we are healed. All of us like sheep have gone astray, each of us has turned to his own way, but the LORD has caused the iniquity of us all to fall on Him. He was oppressed and He was afflicted, yet He did not open His mouth. Like a lamb that is led to slaughter and like a sheep that is silent before its shearers, so He did not open His mouth. By oppression and judgment

He was taken away and as for His generation, who considered that He was cut off out of the land of the living for the transgressions of My people to whom the stroke was due? His grave was assigned with wicked men, yet He was with a rich man in His death, because He had done no violence, nor was there any deceit in His mouth.' (Isaiah 53:1-9)

'But the LORD was pleased to crush Him, putting Him to grief; if He would render Himself as a guilt offering He will see His offspring, He will prolong His days, and the good pleasure of the LORD will prosper in His hand. As a result of the anguish of His soul, He will see it and be satisfied; by His knowledge the Righteous One, My Servant, will justify the many, as He will bear their iniquities. Therefore, I will allot Him a portion with the great, and He will divide the booty with the strong because He poured out Himself to death and was numbered with the transgressors, yet He himself bore the sin of many and interceded for the transgressors.' (Isaiah 53:10-12)

Zechariah looked up to me when he finished reading. His eyes were gaunt and his shoulders slack as if he had received the beatings of the man about whom he just read.

I was numb. I did not want to hear this. We sat in silence and absorbed these words from Isaiah from long ago. I could not think. My head and my heart have never been so heavy. The angel said the baby would reign on the throne of King David and His kingdom will never end. Isaiah said He will bring light into darkness and that He would break the yoke of the oppressor.

But he also says that He will be stricken, hated, pierced, crushed. What does *'bear the iniquities of us all'* mean?

Zechariah broke into my thoughts. He said, "Joseph, this is what I think some of this means. Just as on the day of Passover we lay hands on the sacrificial lamb and symbolically transfer our sins onto it and then we sacrifice it to God, I see this passage in Isaiah describing the same type of sacrificial 'lamb' so to speak, but he is speaking of this *'chosen One of God.'*" I do not know this for sure but the two sacrifices do seem similar."

I looked up at Zechariah. It is one thing to read this in the scriptures and quite another when you know this baby who will grow up to be this man who will suffer such horrendous atrocities, at the hand of His own people, no less.

I cannot do this. I am completely inept to raise this child. I cannot tell Mary this. It will break her heart. She believes He will be a great king!

"My baby is going to suffer horribly." The words caught in my throat and brought tears to my eyes. "And it looks like it is a plan from God, His Father? How can God allow this?

We sat in silence for a long time. We could feel the heaviness of the scriptures weighing on our shoulders, weighing down my heart. I am not sure I needed to hear this. I wish I did not know this. This was written hundreds of years ago. And now it is going to happen to our baby,

Mary's baby.

Zechariah reached across the table and patted my hand. He had no words of consolation; there was nothing he could say to relieve my breaking heart. It was foretold by God, it would happen just as He said.

Just then Elizabeth came into the house carrying John. She placed him in his crib and came over to us. She looked at Zechariah, then to me and back to Zechariah. She could sense something disturbing was going on.

"Zechariah!" She admonished, "What have you done to Joseph! He looks beaten down. I have never seen him look so defeated! What are you men talking about? What did you say to him to make him look so bad? Here now Joseph, let me make you feel better and fix you men something to eat."

I could barely concentrate on what Elizabeth was saying or doing. My body felt so heavy I could barely stand up to leave.

I thanked Zachariah for his help, kissed Elizabeth on the cheek and without another word slumped out of their home and headed to mine.

"OH dear God in Heaven!" I prayed as I walked. "What does all this mean? What have I gotten myself into?"

I walked towards Nazareth with my head down, my shoulders sagging. My thoughts were so jumbled I could not think straight.

I was so lost in thought I did not notice or greet the passerby's. I shuffled my feet in the dusty path hoping that they knew the way home. It was a cold cloudy day. It was exactly how I felt. Then I felt the sting of tears well up in my eyes. I cannot remember the last time I cried. I was so ashamed. I quickly looked around to see if anyone saw me wipe my eyes. I saw a ray of light through the blur of the tears. I looked up and expected to see the clouds parting and a sliver of sun shining down. But it wasn't.

I stopped abruptly. Wiping my running nose with my sleeve I looked up and there was the same angel as before. I think it was the same one. Do they all look the same?

"Joseph," he spoke gently. "Do not be afraid. God is with you and God will be with you. Go in peace." And he was gone.

I looked around to see if anyone else saw the angel. There were a few travelers on the road, but they went about their business as if nothing strange had happened at all. I don't think they saw the angel.

Now I really looked like a fool. Teary eyes, running nose, mouth agape in awe. Someone might look at me and think

I was a mad man.

I sat down on a group of rocks. I had to gather my thought before I got home.

I took a deep breath.

"Ok, God," I muttered to myself. "I trust You, I am honored that You have called me for this indescribably difficult task. Moses complained about his task, but he obeyed You. Gideon had a hard time believing You too, but he did what You asked him to do. And I'm sure Noah was ridiculed and chastised for the role he played in Your great plan."

All will be well. God has a plan for Jesus. It will not change just because I do not understand or because I am in fear of the unknown. But God knows. Jesus is in good hands. Whatever comes our way, God will strengthen us for the task.

I stood up. Straight. Tall. Strong. With another deep breath, I raised my chin, smiled at the passing strangers, squared my shoulders and headed for home. I began to whistle a praise song I remembered from my childhood.

I'll have to teach Jesus how to whistle. And for the first time all day, I laughed out loud.

11

JOSEPH

I could not get Zechariah's words out of my head. Actually I suppose they were Isaiah's words, God's words. What a horrifying description of the abuse. Were those really prophetic words about the Christ, about Jesus? How did Isaiah know?

Of Course? God told Isaiah to write them. God is sending His Son to endure such hardship? Why? How can one prophecy call the Christ Wonderful Counselor, Mighty God, Prince of Peace; and the next one say that He will be despised and forsaken of men, a man of sorrows and acquainted with grief, and like one from whom men hide their face? He will be despised, and we will not esteem Him. It will be God's will to crush Him and make Him suffer.

All I could think about from the last week was my visit with Zechariah. Thank You, God, that I had someone to turn to and explain scripture to me.

Not only was my head spinning with prophecy but my heart was aching for Mary. I knew she is suffering at the hand, or should I say the tongue, of the townspeople. How could people be so vicious? What made them think they have any right to say such malicious things to her? Those self righteous, spiteful people! The rabbi told everyone at the temple that God had visited Mary, but no one believed him. I'm not sure he believed it. I think they are jealous. "Why wasn't my daughter chosen?" I heard a few of those old bitties say. They are white washed tombs. Nice and clean on the outside but full of dead men's bones on the inside.

I was also consumed with the prophesy of the Christ being born in Bethlehem. How am I supposed to get Mary to Bethlehem? We don't know the exact time of the birth. Are we supposed to go and just wait? What would I do for work? I don't have enough money to go and sit in another town and not work.

Then yesterday a Roman stranger came into town. I was told he went right to the temple and asked to see the leaders of the town. Now I can't say he 'asked' because he spoke a different language. He did know the one Hebrew word 'leader'. He found the council gathered in the atrium of the temple. I was told he handed them a scroll and then left.

Hezekiah, the chief counsel, read the decree from Caesar Augustus. It said that Caesar had proclaimed a census and that he demanded that every man must be registered in the empire. Each man over the age of twenty was to go to the town of his ancestors and be registered.

My hometown is Bethlehem. Is this a coincidence? I did not ask Mary when she thought the baby would be born, but it takes nine months, right?

I was stunned by this course of action. How could God prophesy that the Christ will be born in Bethlehem, and then Caesar order a census for me to go to Bethlehem? This was weird.

I went to Mary's house before I went to the carpenters shop this morning. She looked terrible. I had enough presence of mind not to say that out loud but boy, did she look dreadful. Her eyes were puffy and bloodshot and she was so pale. She didn't speak much nor look me in the face. I wonder if someone had said something horrible to her. Probably so. The townspeople were unspeakably cruel. People thought I was crazy for proceeding with the marriage. Why can't God just zap them into understanding? He certainly had the power. He also has the power to smite them. I let my thoughts wander in revenge.

I spoke with Eli about the census. He of course was among the leaders at the temple when the Roman courier arrived.

He thought it was a divine coincidence too. He said he would help me secure a donkey on which Mary could ride and carry our provisions for the trip. There were other people who needed to go to Bethlehem or to a nearby town and we would join the caravan. We would leave in two days.

How is Mary going to endure such a long journey? I am so thankful that we will have help along the way.

Eli will have to go to Bethlehem too, of course. My father Jacob will join the caravan. I heard there were nearly thirty people going. My uncle Hezron will join us from Japha, the next town. Someone estimated that it would be well over 100 miles. We have to navigate through two mountain ranges of Mt. Tabor and Mt. Gilboa. The leaders of the caravan think we should head east from Nazareth and head for Agrippina and stay to the foothills of Tabor and Gilboa as much as possible. We would be wise to follow the Jordan River south so we have fresh water. We certainly want to avoid Samaria as much as possible. Those savages would be all too eager to raid our caravan. We will have to travel a good distance out of the way to avoid Samaria and then head west to Bethlehem.

Not many women are going. Only men have to register, but some women are coming to cook. They expect the journey to take four or five days. FOUR OR FIVE DAYS!! Can you imagine traveling that far just to sign a document and be counted? If Caesar sent messengers, why didn't he just count the people while he was here? What an incredible waste of time! Those darn Romans don't care what they do to the people. Their only concern is to expand the empire. It does not matter the cost to the people of the empire! They don't care. Greedy vipers! I pray God's greatest judgment on them all! I pray God sends plagues like in Egypt. Yea, and leprosy! I hope God makes Caesar and all those blasted senators live a long and painful life with leprosy. That will teach them to mess with God's chosen people! HA!

I was so lost in my vengeful plan to rid our land of the nasty Romans that I did not hear Eli come up to me.

"Joseph" Eli called out. "Are you thinking about Mary and the baby? It will be a very strenuous trip. I sure hope God knows what He is doing by asking Mary to travel so far in her delicate state."

Eli knew the Micah prophesy of the Christ being born in Bethlehem Ephrathah. It is an uncanny coincidence.

I have brought extra money to buy the two pigeons or turtle doves that will be required at the temple for the burnt offering and peace offering for Mary's purification thirty-three days after Jesus is born. Surely we will be able to find a rabbi to circumcise Jesus on the eighth day. I will trust God also to find work for me while we stay the thirty odd days according to the law of purification. I can't worry about that now. No sense borrowing tomorrow's troubles.

Speaking of borrowing.

Eli found a donkey that we could borrow. No way could Mary walk that far. We had to take more provisions that the others because we plan to stay longer. Mary will have to pack blankets and baby items. We might as well plan that the baby will be born while we are there.

I will trust that all will go well. When I am afraid I will trust in Thee. The story of Joshua came to my mind. After Moses died, God chose Joshua to be the leader of the Israelites and lead them into the promise land. Joshua must have been a bit afraid because God told him, "Have I not commanded you? Be strong and courageous, for the LORD your God will be with you wherever you go."

(Joshua 1:9)

If God promised to be with Joshua when he was doing God's will, then I will take that promise also and be strong and courageous in doing God's will.

LUKE 2:4-5 "SO JOSEPH ALSO WENT UP FROM THE TOWN OF NAZARETH IN GALILEE TO JUDEA, TO BETHLEHEM THE TOWN OF DAVID, BECAUSE HE BELONGED TO THE HOUSE AND LINE OF DAVID. HE WENT THERE TO REGISTER WITH MARY, WHO WAS PLEDGED TO BE MARRIED TO HIM AND WAS EXPECTING A CHILD.

12

HANNAH

My heart was heavy with the thought of Mary and Joseph traveling that great distance in Mary's condition. What if she can't make it? What if she is slow and the caravan won't wait for them?

OH Hannah, I admonished myself. There I go worrying again. Praise God that Eli, Joseph and his father Jacob will be with them to help. He was taking our donkey and small cart to carry the provisions and for Mary to ride in when needed.

I helped Mary pack food and purchase as many wine skins as we could find to carry drinking water. We would have to pack some food for the beasts of burden too. I quickly finished embroidering the blanket for the baby the night before. We packed some cloths for diapers and a few pieces of clothing. I knew Mary would be gone for at least thirty days until the end of her purification. If she were having a baby girl, it would be sixty days that she would be considered unclean by the law of Moses. (Leviticus 12:4)

I prayed that Joseph would find work right away while they stayed and waited for the time to pass. What a joy to think that the baby will be presented to and circumcised in the beautiful temple in Jerusalem. I hear it is not as grand as the temple Solomon built but if King Herod did anything right, it was to rebuild the temple to some semblance of grandeur.

The caravan met on the second day just as planned. I had prepared a hearty breakfast for Eli, Jacob, Mary and Joseph and packed up the leftovers. I gathered with them at the grove of trees at the south end of town. There were about forty men and I counted only seven women. The men were not pleased at all that Joseph and Eli were bringing Mary. They knew she would be an encumbrance and possibly cause the caravan to move more slowly than they wanted. They seemed to lose sight of the prophesy of the Christ being born in Bethlehem. They really did not believe that Mary was this fulfillment. If it happened to someone else in another town, perhaps they would believe. But a prophet has no honor in his own town.

There were to be four men who would lead the caravan-Joash the son of Abithar, Ziba the son of Azar, Jonathon the son of Eliakim, and Hushai the son of Perez. I had watched those boys grow up to be men in our town, and I knew Mary and Eli would be in good hands. They came from decent, hard-working families and were skilled and experienced men to command the troops. They were very adept in traveling and knew how to navigate the unsafe roads in Samaria. It was quite the rag-tag group-some on horses, some with small carts, some with donkeys like Mary and Joseph and some walking. That pretty much showed the picture of the socio-economic makeup of the company. The strong ones led the way and the weaker ones brought up the rear, just like the Israelites when they left Egypt. I hoped no one will attack the infirmed that lag behind like the Amalekites did. What a horrible thought!! Please God protect them. Be their rear guard.

The good byes were short and sweet. The women and family members left behind knew they would see their men in ten days or so. But I knew I would not see Mary and the baby for more than thirty days. Eli said he would stay and help them settle into Bethlehem and then find a group to travel back to Nazareth. It was too far and too unsafe for a man, let alone an old man, to travel alone.

"Let's head out!," shouted Joash. I was, or had been good friends with his mother until she joined the other women passing judgment about Mary's pregnancy. Still, I had to concede that she raised her son to be an accomplished young man. He was a valiant warrior and was adept at defending against an enemy or killing an animal for food with his sword. I did feel better knowing Eli, Mary and Joseph were in his competent charge.

They divided the travelers in groups of tens. Hushai took the lead and the first ten followed. Then Ziba fell into line with another ten or so. Joash accompanied the next ten, and Jonathon brought up the rear and those that remained.

The children and I stood at the grove and waved and watched the procession. Mary and Joseph were among the last group. We watched until they were out of sight. I wanted desperately to go with them but I knew I had to stay with the rest of the children. With a big sigh of resignation to this fact, I gathered the children and began to walk home. The two youngest boys ran towards home playing some sort of game among the trees and boulders that only children seem to be able to create out of nothing. Zipporah and I walked home in silence. I wonder what was going through her mind? Did she have any idea of the life- changing events that were just set into motion? The Savior of the world would be born soon.

The greatest prophesy of God was about to be fulfilled.

13

MARY

I was very excited but apprehensive about the trip. It was quite a crowd that had gathered that morning to see all of us off. Mama had packed us lots of food. I know she wanted to come with us. I promised her I would find a midwife as soon as I arrived in Bethlehem. She wanted to be there to help me but she had to stay with the other children. I know her heart was torn in two. I wanted her to be with me. I needed her help.

She told us over and over that we would be fine and that I was young and strong and would be able to weather the trip without much hardship.

"Just remember," she told me, "when it gets so bad

that you think you can take another step, it will get worse."

Oddly enough, I found those words to be tremendously comforting. Mama was a rock. She was the toughest woman I knew both physically and mentally. She worked from sun up to sun down and never complained. She always seemed to keep a happy disposition especially when times got tough. It took me years to notice her one daily routine. When she saw Abba turn the corner at the top of the street and head home at the end of the day, she would inconspicuously disappear. She would return to the kitchen and I noticed her hair had been brushed and pinned back up, and she had rubbed some scented oil on her neck. She would nibble on some fresh herbs to make her breath smell fresh. She and Abba had the best marriage I had ever seen. Abba was not like some of the men who did not respect the women in their lives. They treated their wives harshly and their daughters like servants. I cringed when I would see that behavior in town and feel so bad for the women. Those men treated their animals better than their wives and daughters.

I am glad I have such good role models in my life. I know Joseph loves and respects me and will always treat me with kind loving hands. He loved his mother. I would see them occasionally around town together. He was a very dutiful son. He always walked beside her and carried her bags. When he was younger, I heard that some of his friends called him a 'mama's boy. Huh, all because he showed love and respect for her. When she died suddenly, he was devastated. All of the men in that family lost the light of their lives. Jacob has never fully recovered. He seems happy but not joyful. They did not have daughters so it was extra tough to keep the house a home. I know now that Joseph and his brothers sought out certain characteristics in their wives that reminded them of their mother. I have big shoes to fill. I am honored that Joseph sees something in me that reminds him of his mother. For that I am very grateful.

So these were my thoughts as we began our 100-mile journey. Nazareth had long ago dropped out of sight. Joseph and I were among the group that brought up the rear. I was delighted to see my energy was high and I was not holding the group behind. The foreman seemed to have settled into a routine-travel for about two hours and then stop to rest and get water. They stayed to this pattern for the first day. I walked a surprising part of the day and rode the donkey some. The donkey was not very comfortable. I never was tired enough to ride in Abba's cart. I will save that for last extremes.

The countryside was beautiful. The sun made the rocks of the mountains change colors as it moved across the sky. We did have some sort of path that we were following. It was relatively smooth and that made for easy walking for the animals and us. The weather was on our side too. The day started cool, and as we stayed at the base of the mountains and headed east towards the Jordan River, it grew more and more lush and green. We could feel the moisture in the air too. Funny how water lifts your spirits when you are tired. Even the beasts of burden picked up the pace as we neared the Jordan.

Joash was the foreman of our group. He and Joseph had known each other for a long time and had done business together. Joseph was much older than he and had a great respect for Joash. He was secure in his ability to lead us safely to Bethlehem. Mama and Joash's mother were friends, and I think they had their sights set on Joash and me getting married. Joash was not for me. I had seen the way he treated children and old people when he thought no one was looking. He had a distrustful look in his eye like he thought the world owed him something that he was not getting. He might be good at his job and trustworthy on the trail but his home life might be a different story. Thank God Abba did not betroth me to him. Joseph was the right choice. Yes, he was considerably older than I was, but that was very common. More of my friends married older men than those who married men closer to their age.

Joash and the other foremen were riding horses and had gathered together to establish our first campsite. They had taken this route before and had favorite pre-established landmarks. If the caravan moved quickly they have certain spots, but if it moved slowly like we had, they have alternate sites picked out. They began to move the caravan towards the base of the mountain that had a natural cleft. It had rock walls on three sides and would block the wind if it would gust up from the west heading to the river. It was an alcove honed by centuries of wind whipping at the rock. The opening faced southwest.

As we circled up into the cove we stayed in our traveling groups. I was told this would be easier to protect us and keep the group warm or cool depending on our needs. The first course of business was to fan out and gather firewood while we still had daylight. Joseph and I walked together, and I filled his arms and then lay what I could carry in my apron. My swollen belly did not leave much depth for the apron, but I could hold it out as far as my arms could reach. I was not going to let anyone say that I did not carry my load. I knew by the looks on their faces and their nasty comments that they made while I was in earshot, that they were none too pleased that I was traveling with them. I might as well have been a cripple for the contemptuous looks I got from them.

I would use Joseph to shield me from them. I don't know if Joseph knew what I was doing but he provided a soothing buffer between those spiteful people and me. Most of the vicious comments came from the women. Women can be so catty.

Joseph and I stayed to ourselves. We built a small fire to take the chill out of the air. He unloaded the blankets and made up two beds next to each other. Mama packed food that we could eat cold and not have to cook. I cut up some bread and some cheese. We ate the fruit tonight so it would not go bad. I secretly packed a few treats of dates and raisins and almonds. After our simple dinner, we reclined on our blankets. I reached into the leather pouch I had hidden in the roll of blankets and put some of the date mixture in my hands.

I scooted over to Joseph and opened my hand. The look

on his face was priceless and worth the extra cost of these delicacies. He had the most remarkable smile. He still had all his teeth and they were surprisingly white. He had the kind of smile that lit up his whole face. It actually made his eyes sparkle. His laugh came easy and everyone who met him or spent time with him was better for it. His words were always positive and he looked for the best in people. He was always the first to lend a helping hand and would give his time and talent to those in need. Many girls hoped to marry him. It was shameful to see how many of those girls flaunted themselves at him after his mother passed away. They were trying to 'soothe' him. HA! They were trying to manipulate him when he was at a weak moment. Those scanks. Joseph reached out and cupped my hand in his. "Thank you Mary, dates are my favorite."

No kidding, I smiled! Like I didn't know his every like and dislike. I had been studying Joseph for years. I knew he prefers a dinner of lamb over beef. He likes his meat heavily peppered. He will do anything for a glass of warm goat's milk. He always sits on the left side second row at temple. He rises before dawn, drinks a large glass of water and spends time worshiping God in private. He then eats the same thing for breakfast every morning and packs a few things for lunch. He always cleans his tools at the end of the day and lays them in a perfect row on his workbench or hangs them up on pegs. He sweeps the sawdust into a shallow bowl and carries it to his mother's flowerbeds. She said it helped keep the moisture in the ground and help the flowers grow stronger. When he is stressed, he will take his mat and head up to the hill on the north side of town and watch the stars for hours. There are fewer trees on that side of Nazareth and it gives him a wider view of the heavens. He took me there a few times. He wasn't stressed, I might add. He just wanted to share his 'private spot of serenity' with me.

I looked into his deep brown eyes as he reached up for the treat. He hands were surprisingly warm. They were very rough and callused but warm. They told me that he works hard and that he will work hard for our family and me. I have seen him with only his tunic on and his bare arms showing. OH MY! Was he strong! He had huge forearms and very muscular biceps! His shoulders were broad and well developed. I stood in the doorway of his shop admiring my future husband for several minutes before he knew I was there. The few times we have been alone I found myself melting into his arms as he hugged me. Sometimes as he wrapped me in his arms, I would imagine it was God holding me and protecting me. At times I would lay my head on his chest and I could hear his heart beat. Thump thump, thump thump, thump thump. Strong, constant, steady. Just like Joseph.

"I'm going to talk with some of the men about the journey. Will you be okay here by yourself?"

He helped me to my feet. OH, I should not have sat so long! All my joints and muscles were starting to feel the demand I had placed on them today. I felt bigger now than when I started the day if THAT was possible! HOW CAN I GET SO

BIG? Will I ever look normal again? I stretched my hands over my head. My body was not happy with me. I rested them on the small of my back, a pose I find myself striking more and more.

"I'll be fine. I'm going to lie down and I'm sure I will fall asleep immediately."

"Ok dear, I won't be long." Joseph kissed me on the top of my head and left.

I stoked the fire and spread it out to encourage it to die out. I lay on my left side and pulled the blanket over my shoulders.

"Thank you, God, for giving me extra energy today. Thank you for seeing us through the first day. I know You are with us every step. Please, please God, help me get through these next miles. Help me to have a good attitude and not complain. You are my shield and my very great reward. I love You."

I knew I was in dreamland before the last syllable left my lips.

14

JOSEPH

The night before we headed out, a group of men that will be part of the caravan and I met with Jonathon, Joash, Ziba and Hushai, the four foremen. My father met with us. He, too, must register in Bethlehem. It was a great source of relief knowing that he and my brothers will be with me to help with Mary. The four guides were experienced men and had led a number of trips to different parts of Israel. The Roman government was harsh on us with taxes but left us alone and allowed us to live by the laws of Moses and travel freely within the boundaries of Israel. I had been on many of these excursions with Eliab and Kish and sometimes with other friends. I loved traveling on the open road. I loved camping under the stars and living off the land. Some people thought I should become a foreman, but I could never leave Father. Especially now that Mother is gone. I had grown up with these four men and gladly put Mary and myself into their capable hands. These men were swift with a sword and could drop a mountain lion with a bow and arrow at 100 paces. If there were food to be had along the trail, they would bag it and cook it up!

Eliab laid out the route and assured us that they had already established the campsites. They hoped to make Bethlehem in 4 days. Jonathon made suggestions on what and how much to pack. They cannot be sure there will be enough firewood so we should be prepared to pack foods that do not need to be cooked.

After the meeting a few of us men stood around outside the building and exchanged packing strategies, which pack animal to take and simply shoot the breeze. I had known these people all my life. There was not a stranger among us. They were concerned for Mary's safety and comfort. I'm not sure how many of them believed that Mary's baby was indeed from God. I know that Eliab and Kish had my back. They knew me too well that I would never do something like that. And truthfully, other than my father, no one's opinion mattered.

I woke up the next morning before the sun popped its head above the horizon. I loved road trips and was keyed up to get this one started. I tried not to think about the event in store for us in Bethlehem. I decided I would just follow Mary's lead. Her mother surely gave her advice on how to birth, the baby and Mary had been with Elizabeth with her birth so she should be somewhat prepared. I never had a sister so I have no clue about women things.

We all gathered at the cluster of sycamore trees on the south end of town. The foreman divided us up in groups, and without fanfare we headed out. Mary and I did not speak much for the first few miles. I kept a wary eye on her for fatigue or pain or any discomfort. She surprised me! What a trouper she turned out to be! She quickly found a rhythm to her gait, and if you had not looked past her shoulders you would never guess she was nine months pregnant.

We stopped about every two hours to rest and get water. I thought we were moving along vigorously for being such a large group. I was going over the checklist in my head of the things I must do once we arrived in Bethlehem. The first thing would be to register, of course, and then I must secure some place for us to stay temporarily. The law stated that Mary would be unclean for thirty-three days, and then on the eighth day after Jesus' birth He must be circumcised. I had saved up a little money but I will need to find work right away. Father said he would stay long enough to make sure we get settled in. We will need two pigeons or doves as a burnt offering for Mary's purification. That should not be difficult to procure. We bought things for the baby so there should be no expense incurred. Mary said she would seek out a midwife as soon as we get to Bethlehem.

Just as we were getting ready to leave, Hannah pressed two

gold coins into my hand. "Take care of my little girl." She said with tears in her eyes. She hugged me furiously for several minutes. I wrapped my arms around her and tried to absorb some of her grief. With a huge sigh, she released me and returned to the waiting children. I know this was not the circumstance under which she visualized Mary's first born to arrive. But her heart was overflowing knowing that her baby girl was the fulfillment of scripture.

The cool morning quickly gave way to the warm afternoon sun. We allowed the sun to rise in silence over the Jordan River. We were approaching the foothills of Mt. Tabor and Mt. Gilboa that towered above us. I had to hand it to the Romans. They had carved out some roads through the empire. It did make travel much easier. I understand that the road that follows the Jordan River was wide and remarkably flat and free of debris. As we crested a ridge, the path that we had been taking around the foothills led us directly east towards the Jordan. We could smell the river before we could see it. The humidity in the air changed and we were excited to get to the water and refresh ourselves. To Mary's frustration, we had been instructed to halt for rest and water our animals. We were still in the cool shadow of the mountains and I gazed back at them and chuckled at the analogy of those mountains to the mountainous task I was asked by God to climb. As I was contemplating the upcoming unknown events, God brought to mind a psalm.

"I lift my eyes to the hills, where does my help come from?
My help comes from the LORD, the Maker of heaven and

earth. He will not let your foot slip; He who watches over you will not slumber. Indeed He who watches over Israel will neither slumber nor sleep. The LORD watches over you, the LORD is your shade at your right hand; the sun will not harm you by day or the moon by night. The LORD will keep you from all harm, He will watch over your life. The LORD will watch over your coming and your going both now and forevermore. (Psalm 121).

"Thank you God for those comforting words." I mumbled.

"Are you alright?" Mary looked up at me in concern.

"God is good, ya know." I stared at her with a half smile playing at the corner of my mouth.

Then as the Word of God soared in my head as a mighty eagle in flight, a full on smile ascended across my face. "Everything will be okay." I assured her.

Break time was over. I playfully squirted some water on Mary's head. She let out a yelp and thumped me on the chest in good spirits. Mary was good at taking a joke. She could take it as well as dish it out. I think my love grew for her a little more during that good -humored exchange.

We pulled the feedbag from our donkey, stowed our water pouches and headed towards the river. The land had become flat, and my mind was free to wander and not pay such close attention to the trail. I watched Mary amble in front of me. I remember the first time I laid eyes on her. Mother had met Hannah at the well many years ago. Her oldest daughter Tamar was approaching marrying age, and the two women schemed of marrying her off to me. My mother was constantly singing the praises of Tamar. If we saw her in the market place, Mother would nudge me to go speak to her. I obliged her and made small talk with Tamara a few times, but I did not get the sense that she was interested in me. Truth be known, I felt no inkling toward her either. She was cute and all from what I could see behind her veil, but there was no zing factor. That is Eliab used to call it. And believe me, Eliab had an eye for a beautiful woman with zing. It drove his parents crazy! They should have named him Samson, because he had become a womanizer just like the old judge of Israel.

After the third time of speaking with Tamar, I told Mother that I was not interested in her and asked her kindly to stop the match making. I was old enough to pick my own wife now. I will accept her opinion, but no more pushing. She politely acquiesced. She wanted a daughter-in-law in the worse way. She longed to share the mother/daughter bond. I was the oldest of my brothers and was expected to marry first. But work with my father took precedence over my love life, and my brother Nehemiah got married first and then Jethro. People were starting to call me a confirmed bachelor.

Then came that wonderful, fateful spring day when I was

out of the carpenter shop heading for Nebat's. Father needed some tanning oil to stain a piece of wood on which he was working. I wasn't watching where I was going. Something caught my eye in the sky. A smaller bird was chasing a considerably larger bird who had a horrible shrill of a voice. I had a feeling that the larger bird had been robbing the nest of the smaller bird. David and Goliath can be found throughout the animal kingdom, I guess.

I was in a hurry to get back to the shop and turned the corner and ran right into a young girl carrying two clay water pots on a pole across her shoulders. I hit her full on. She staggered back and tottered to her right swinging the pole and pots full of water. She overcompensated and leaned too far left in an attempt to balance herself and the pot on the left side slid off the pole and crashed to the ground. Now unbalanced she teetered to the right again and the momentum turned her a full 180 degrees and the clay pot on the right side swung sideways and THUD! Hit me square in my back. The force sent me flying forward with hand splayed out and I landed with a solid HUMPH! On my chest.

I lay in stunned disbelief with a mouth full of Israeli sand and the dust rising up to my eyes. My beard was quickly being caked with mud as the dirt mixed with my spittle. My eyes naturally began to water to remove the dust and my nose began to run. I took a quick survey as to which hurt more. My chest or my back or my pride?

I gathered my wits and rose to my hands and knees. WHACK! I felt a stab of pain across my backside! I fell prostrate to the earth and quickly rolled over to face my assailant. It was that little girl! She hit me! She was pointing her pole towards me like a jouster. I could not see her face through her veil but her eyes told me she meant business. She had a crazed glare like a wild cat cornered by menacing boys with a gunnysack. This girl was hardly 5 feet tall and under all those robes I knew she could not be 100 pounds. But she made up for her small stature in chutzpa. I tried not to laugh. I lifted my hand to my mouth with the pretense of wiping off the dirt but really it was to hide my smile.

"Are you crazy?" She barked at me. "What! Do you think you own these streets and don't have to watch where you are going? Look what you did to my pots! My water is spilled all over. If I get in trouble, I'm going to find you and make you pay!"

I was speechless. Kids these days. Where did she learn such spunk? I started to rise to my feet, brushing off my tunic when I noticed another pair of small feet behind the robed wildcat.

"Com'n Mary," the smaller one was pulling on the taller one's clothes. "Let's get home. Mama won't yell. It was an accident."

Mary, I presumed, turned to me and lunged at me one last time with her pole/jouster, just to show me that she was not afraid of me. Then the masked spitfire ran off, pole tightly clenched in her hands.

"Geesh, Joseph," I heard someone say. "Having a little trouble with the ladies? It seems to me that it is a perfectly beautiful day to ruin it making enemies!"

A small group had gathered when the commotion started. I bent over to pick up the broken pottery. I was still trying to get the dirt off my face and out of my eyes. I squinted to make my eyes water and wash the dirt away. How could a small girl make such a mess of me?

I tossed the pieces into the trash pile and remembered to find my oil. Good thing it was in a leather pouch and did not break open when I took my first plunge.

I headed back to the shop wondering who was that veiled vixen? DANG! What a whole lot of woman! Now that was my kind of gal!

The memory made me bust out laughing! Mary turned to me with the 'are you crazy' look.

"I was just thinking about the first time we met, when you hit me with your water pots."

"I HIT YOU?" Mary said incredulously. "You plowed right into me and never even apologized!"

"You never gave me a chance. Besides, I was too busy trying not to laugh at the sight of you and that pole. I thought you were going to impale me."

"I would have too, if I thought I wouldn't get blood on my robe." Mary said with a twinkle in her eye.

"That is the day I knew you were the one for me."

"Yea, yea, yea. That is what all the boys said." I could tell she was smiling behind her veil.

"Oh, so there were a lot of boys who wanted your hand in marriage?"

"Abba said he could not remember all their names so he had to give them numbers." She said as she tossed her scarf over her should in a "look at me, I'm special' stance. "You were insufferable. Did you pay off Abba to get rid of the other boys?" Her repartee voice drenching her words.

Mary did play hard to get.

After the broken water pots fiasco, it took me several days to find out who she was. Then I was on my way to the temple and saw her with Tamar and wondered if she was her younger sister all grown up? It had been several years since my mother's failed match-making attempt with Tamar. This couldn't be that tomboy Mary? I used to watch her play with the boys when her mother wasn't watching. She had an incredibly accurate slingshot. Must run in the family. She could out-run most of the boys too.

If I did my math right, Mary should be a young woman now and not the young girl that she appears to be. It is tough to tell the age of a woman when you can only see her eyes.

"I told you the story a hundred times, Mary."

"I'm sure I don't remember." Her teasing voice drifting back to me. "Tell me again. How did you get Abba to agree to our engagement?"

"Actually my dear, Eli approached me. He knew his tomboy, wildcat of a daughter needed an older man to settle her down. He knew a boy closer to your age did not have the wisdom or demeanor to handle a young woman as mischievous as yourself."

"OH, SO I'M A HANDFUL NOW, AM I?"

Not sure if I heard sarcasm or anger?

"For pete sakes, Mary, you know you could chew them up and spit them out."

"I can play the docile wife." Mary said trying to reassure herself, or was it me, of her proper role.

"Yes, dear, whatever you say."

Our banter of words was a game of sport, like a ball being tossed back and forth. We knew the game well, and like any good athlete we watched for an open opportunity in the conversation to slam dunk the ball in the opponent's court and win the 'game'. That was the perfect analogy of our relationship. We were very playful with each other and enjoyed our competitiveness.

Just as Mary opened her mouth to reply, Joash called for a halt in the caravan. "Saved by the bell." I said. Once in a great while I will take the game too far and hurt Mary's feelings. I promised myself I would never make her cry again like I had when she told me about the baby. I will learn to control my tongue and not press her too hard with my teasing.

She was so much fun to be with. I can't wait to be married and be alone with each other.

I think my love for her just grew a little more.

The day had passed remarkably fast and it was time to make camp. Mary was beginning to look a bit weary so camp came none too soon.

The foremen had picked another protective spot close to the river.

I took the donkey and tied her up with the rest of the beasts and grabbed our packs. I laid out the blankets so Mary could rest comfortably while I went back to feed the donkey.

When I returned, she had prepared some dinner for us. The bread was beginning to become stale but I did not complain. We had some matzo crackers for the last two days so I could suffer through this meal. She cut open a pomegranate and plucked out the seeds. The burst of flavor was an exciting treat. We ate up the last of the meat, not daring to keep it in the sun for a third day. Hannah had dried it in salt brine but we could not gamble on eating bad meat. The next two days will be cheese and the matzo. Wouldn't it be nice if it rained manna and quail? I would not complain like our forefathers did.

We did not make a fire, but were kept comfortable by the warm westerly breeze like a breath from God.

Mary and I snuggled up together on the padded blankets leaning against the rocks of protection around us. We watched the sun drop below the horizon and bid a farewell, a chairo to a superb day. *Thou, O LORD, did make the dawn and sunset shout for joy,* (Psalm 66:8) I prayed in thanksgiving.

The moon gave permission to the night sky to open its arms to the heavens and let the stars take the stage for their evening performance.

I could tell by Mary's rhythmic breathing that she had fallen asleep. I gently laid her on her side, propped her head under a small pillow and covered her shoulders with a blanket.

I curled up to her as close as I dared. I wrapped myself in the blanket of God's peace and love and fell asleep before my head hit my pillow.

15

MARY

I sat up slowly. I had not remembered falling asleep. The last thing I did was to lay my head on Joseph's shoulder and feel the warm breeze on my face. Now my body was defying my command to stand and get moving.

Every muscle ached. I looked at my hands. They looked like ten cucumbers! I could hardly bend them they were so swollen. My skin was pulled so tight that it almost looked shiny. The dirt embedded in my fingernails and cuticles almost disappeared by the overstuffed skin around my nail beds.

I took inventory of the rest of my body. My forearms were bloated, my back felt like it was on fire because of the muscle fatigue. I could hardly sit up straight because my shoulders throbbed. I looked down at my lap and pulled my robe up a little to see my legs.

"AHH!" I yelled in shocked disbelief! My ankles were as big as my knees! My legs were the same size from my knees to my feet! My feet looked like stuffed olives with ten itty bitty pieces of garlic sticking out! I was horrified! What has happened to my body?!

I struggled to my knees. With tremendous effort I put one foot flat on the ground and propped myself with my hands on the bent knee. A loud groan catapulted me to both feet and I stood up with a grunt. I swooned with a light head and saw stars dancing before my eyes. I almost fell backwards, and all that effort to stand erect would have been for naught.

"OH GOODNESS!" What is wrong with me? My belly hurt in the worst way too. I don't know if it was my imagination, but the baby seemed to be lower on my hips. It always looked as if it were a small soft melon attached to my rib cage. Now it seemed so low. I touched it. It felt so much firmer as well. My upper arms and chest felt more tender too. There was pain shooting down the inside of my arms from my armpits to my elbows.

I was an absolute mess! Joseph does not want a weak woman, especially weak woman the size of an ox! At least an ox is good for something!

"Okay, Mary," I said to myself, "Pull yourself together! Mama told you to drink plenty of water to help with the swelling. She didn't mention the soreness that accompanied the bloating." Geez, now I know how the fatted calf feels waiting before the banquet. All plump and juicy and ready for the slaughter. Well, not the slaughter part but I did feel plump and juicy. I could press my finger into my arm and leave a dent! It was amazing! I looked like bread dough. I pressed my fingertip into my skin just like I do when I am kneading the dough. My finger shape remains in my skin for several seconds. If I were not in so much pain, it would be funny.

"Will I ever have my old body back?"

I was so engrossed in my alien body that I did not notice Joseph had returned. I can't say I even noticed he was gone. Man, I can be so self absorbed sometimes! What if I am all up in my own business and totally forget where I laid the baby? I am going to be an awful mother. What if I lose the Son of God? Would I go straight to Hades if I could not find Jesus? Would God forgive me? Could God forgive me? Would He ask someone else to have another Son after I failed Him?

Am I going crazy? I am standing here having fun making kneading marks in my skin fretting about misplacing my baby somewhere! I am a nut case! Maybe God will see that He made a mistake choosing me and start all over.

Joseph stood at a cautious ten feet from me, watching the conversation I was having with myself as I poked my skin. He had heard that the heat can do strange things to the mind, but it was not overly hot.

"Mary?" he approached with prudence as one approaches a lunatic. "Mary? Are you okay? Can I help you find something?"

My head shot up and my eyes bulged. How long had he been standing there watching me? He must think I have lost my mind. Have I been speaking out loud or have I had this bizarre conversation in my head?

"Mary?" Joseph had made his way to my side and looked at my dough like arm that was turning red from the obsessive kneading. "Are you talking to someone? Is anything wrong with the baby? You were mumbling something and I heard you say Jesus."

"LOOK AT ME!" Yep, I just took one giant step and fell off the deep end! "I have cucumber fingers, stuffed olives feet, my legs are the same size from the knees to my ankles and my skin looks like bread dough!! My shoulders hurt, my back is on fire and I look like an ox!

I started to sob.

"You can just leave me here! I know you must be embarrassed by my looks!" I managed to sputter those words in between sobs. "I nearly fill out my robe! I bet if you stick a pin in me I would pop!"

Joseph did what he has learned to do best. Just hold me and let me ride out the tidal wave of emotion. I'm mortified to say this is not the first melt down that he had to weather with me. He has gotten good at just holding me close to his chest and waiting for me to expel my hormonal tidalwave.

He did have the patience of Job. Even Abba said that. Abba knew just the kind of husband I needed. Fun, strong, smart and patient.

I inhaled as deep as my squashed lungs could hold and let out a long cleansing breath. One more breath and the raging waters would return to a bubbling brook.

"All better?" Sweet Joseph Job said as he stroked my hair.

"Are you sure you want to marry me? I am a wreck on two feet that look like grapes!"

"I thought they looked like stuffed olives." He said and quickly clamped his hand over his mouth mortified over what he just allowed to sip out. "Sorry."

I glared up at him through my red puffy eyes.

Stay calm Mary, I said to myself. He was only trying to humor you out of your ill mood.

A third deep breath and I took a quick assessment of the situation.

This whole thing started with God, an angelic visit, Holy Spirit, a baby whose name will mean 'God with us', my being called favored one, God will be with you, 100-mile journey to a strange place, swollen legs, cucumber fingers, stuffed-grape feet...I mean stuffed olives and...Joseph.

AHHH Joseph. I rubbed my hands up and down his oh-so-strong back. I could feel his well-developed chest under my moist cheek. His strong and muscular arms encircled around my growing body.

And we stood wrapped in each other and in God's love. We took a collective breath together and exhaled slowly.

"All better." I announced. "Thanks for your patience with me."

"Any time." You'll never get rid of me," Joseph joked with me.

"I'd be a fool to try."

I lifted my head to meet his gaze. He wiped away the remaining tears with his two thumbs, one on each side.

"We are good together, ya know," Joseph proclaimed, his voice only above a whisper.

"Yes, sir. I knew what I was doing when I set out my trap to catch you." I tried to act as coy as a schoolgirl.

Joseph lifted his face to the sky and busted out laughing. He gave me as big of a hug as he deemed safe and lifted me off the ground and swung me around.

I landed softly on my squishy grape/olive feet and quickly looked around to see if anyone had been watching us in such a public display of affection.

"Let's pack up." Joseph suggested.

He bent over to roll up our blankets and I walked over to fetch the donkey.

It was promising to be another beautiful day, maybe not weather wise, but emotionally a delightful day. I was carrying the Son of God who would save our people from their sins. What could possibly go wrong?

16

JOSEPH

It did not take long for Mary to become too weak and tired to walk. At the first break for rest and water I went up ahead to find Eli. He had a cart that could be used to carry Mary when she grew weary. Today she grew weary.

Eli broke from his group of the caravan and followed me back with his cart and donkey. Mary was the lone straggler of the last group. Eli ran to his daughter and gave her a fatherly hug and kiss on the forehead. She instantly became his baby girl again. I had turned the donkey and cart to face south and Eli helped Mary into the cart. He had padded the backside with straw and two old blankets.

I could tell by Mary's face that the relief was instant. She lay on her left side on top of the straw and gave her father a weak smile.

"Thank you, Abba." She whispered and then she closed her eyes.

With Mary off of her feet we quickly caught up with the rest of the caravan. We could not afford to be left behind. The dreaded Samaritan area of Israel lay ahead. That was not the place to be caught alone and unguarded.

We would follow the Jordan south and then cut back east and avoid Jericho and the area. It was a difficult decision to leave the comfort of the river and the constant water supply but these were not safe roads. Even for a caravan as large as ours, bandits were a threat.

Hushai, Jonathon and Ziba had gone ahead by several miles to do some reconnaissance. In essence, they paved the way of safety for which the rest of us would pass. With so many travelers bound for Jerusalem and the surrounding area, it would be a great temptation that marauding bandits might find hard to resist. I personally had no sword or knife but I had a long pole about thirty-six inches long and two inches thick. If anyone got near us they would quickly learn how hard and unyielding is a piece of cedar. I may not be skilled with a sword, but I am as strong as any two men combined. I am sure it will not come to that, but I must be prepared. It is not all about me anymore.

128

The day passed quickly and quietly now that Mary was reasonably comfortable in the cart. The road was relatively smooth so it did not jolt her too much. I pulled my donkey to the group ahead of us and walked with my father and Eli and the other men for most of the day. We passed the time with men talk. You know-how the crops were faring, if there had been sufficient rains in the spring to carry us to the second rains of the year. They asked me my opinion on the quality of wood that was coming as far north as Sidon and Tyre. I thought the constant wind from the sea made for a stronger tree thus stronger wood with which to make carts, benches and tables. It was too strong to bend to make wheels and certain tools. My opinion was that the cost was prohibitive for most common projects.

But as usual, talk always came back to the Roman government and the grip it had on our lives. They allowed us enough rope to govern ourselves and to keep with the traditions of our way of worship but if we pushed for freedom to police ourselves and provide our own civil laws, the rope would tighten and hang us.

King Herod was the worse offender. Such a vocalized comment was never spoken out loud for fear of being arrested for treason. He desperately wanted to be more than he really was-a puppet of Caesar Augustus. He tried to buy the respect and adoration of the Roman people as well as the Jews. He built roads, buildings, and water and sewer system. He designed glorious gardens and terraces. His crowning jewel was indeed the temple in Jerusalem. Although it paled in comparison to Solomon's temple, I have been told it was beautiful. However, knowing that it was commissioned to be built by a non-Jew sort of stripped it of its holiness. It almost seemed...unclean. Not to take away any glory of the God of Whom we worshipped in the temple, but I find the whole structure to be...fake. Like you are trying to be good enough, beautiful enough for God to hear you.

I like our simple synagogue back in Galilee. Father and I were commissioned to do some of the woodwork inside. I found myself praying as I carved the scenes around the different altars. When I carve, I feel God's pleasure. I know He has gifted me to work with my hands. I really love what I do. I wish I could do more of it and make a better living and provide for Mary and the upcoming family. I was sure we would have other children than Jesus. God never told us not to, right? If we are to get married then a family is naturally to follow...right?

This was a thought I had not considered until this very moment. I am sure we were permitted to have other children. Unless, of course, Mary becomes barren after this birth. I will raise Jesus as my own, but I know He is not. The message from the angel still throws me for a loop, "And the Holy Spirit will overshadow you and therefore the offspring shall be called the Son of God." I cannot wrap my head around the actuality of it all but I have faith that God knows what He is doing. Me, the father of the Son of God! Will I be permitted to discipline Him? Will He need to be disciplined? How does one go about spanking the Son of God? What a weird thought. I bet in all of Jewish history no one ever had that thought! If we have other children will they know their brother is actually God in the flesh? It would be tough to fight with God. When they play games do they need to let God win? Or will they make Him earn the victory?

This conversation was too bizarre! But real, nonetheless. Jesus will be born a real baby. Nurse, sleep, poop. He will crawl, walk, fall down, skin His knee and bleed.

I presume He will bleed.

He'll grow up, go to school, play around with other boys, go fishing, and climb trees.

Right? He will grow up like a normal boy? Won't He? Why wouldn't He?

Should I teach Him the carpentry trade? Will He even be interested?

What will the Son of God do?

Okay.

My mind was on overload. I have this conversation with myself all the time. I hope Mary knows what she is doing. I can build a crib and make toys but other than that, I don't know how much help I will be. I have held a baby only twice in my entire life! What if I break Him? What if I drop Him? I don't think I can just say, "Oops, sorry, God." Could God forgive me? Would God forgive me if I accidently hurt His Son?

HELP!! I DON'T KNOW WHAT I AM DOING!!

As I was finishing my tirade with myself, the men who were put in charge when the foremen left for reconnaissance called for a water-and-rest break.

Mary had been awake and riding quietly, but she alighted from the cart to stretch and drink some water. She sure was a trooper. She never complained during this trip. We had no idea what lay ahead for us in Bethlehem, but God had helped us so far. I knew Hannah was praying for us. We have one more day until we get there. We made it this far, we can push through.

The deputy foremen gave the signal, and we were on the road again, like a band of gypsies we roll down the highway. Mary chose to walk with me. The men I had been traveling with had started at a quicker pace, so within several minutes they were ahead of us, and we found ourselves towards the back of the pack...again.

The respite in the back of the cart revived Mary

tremendously. Her gait was brisk, well... brisk for a woman in her condition. I know it killed her to be in this precarious state. She was such a strong, take charge kind of woman that admitting to any weakness or limitation did not set well with her character. She swallowed her pride more than once and asked me for help with the simplest tasks. She does not know that I love to serve her. I am not like most men my age who treat their women like property, like a second-class citizen.

My father treated my mother like a queen. She worked very hard in the house and in the carpenter shop. She helped father haul wood and sand the finishing pieces. She kept the shop clean, too. She actually taught him to clean his tools every night and lay them in a row for the next day's work. I even do that now. He would build her beautiful things for our home. Some of them were practical pieces like a hand-carved chest for blankets, boxes with hidden hinges in which to store food to keep the sand and bugs out and ornately impressed hooks to hang our outer garment when we entered the house.

Then there were the gorgeous pieces that were fine works of art that held no purpose save to make one appreciate the exquisite wood and artwork. She displayed them proudly and her friends secretly envied the extravagance. In a land where prudence was king, these tokens of affection were a valued prize. One could look at the years of gifts and see how father's skill had improved. The tall, carved vase held a spot of honor on the sideboard in the front room. She filled it with flowers as often as she could find them. In the winter, mother had the canny knack of arranging twigs and pine boughs into attractive arrangements that did not need flowers.

Mother was wonderful. She worked hard and played hard. She never cared what the other women thought of her as she played with us boys. She played all kinds of games with us. She could kick a ball like a boy. Once she showed us how she could kick the hacky sack with either foot. She taught us games that she played as a child. She grew up with all brothers and did not care too much for housework. She would tell us stories of sneaking out of the house to run and play with her brothers. Once in a while they would reciprocate and help her with some of her work so she would not get into trouble.

She made it clear to us early on that because there was no daughter in the house we boys must chip in and help. Father backed her 100% and did not think it was an affront to our masculinity to sweep the floor occasionally. We knew if we wanted mother and father to join us and make the two teams have an even number of players then we had to help out and lighten her work load.

Funny the things you think of on a long trip. I had not thought of the family games we played for along time. I vowed right there that Jesus would have a fun family life. We would teach him to work hard and play hard. Laughter is good medicine. Mary was a good sport and she would see to it that her children have a full enjoyable life.

"What are you smiling about?" Mary stared at me quizzically.

"Thinking about my mother. You remind me a lot of her."

I could see Mary blush even under the veil.

"I'm glad. Thank you. I have been told she was a very special woman. I have never heard anyone speak an unkind word about her. And believe you me, if someone had an unkind word, they would speak it." Mary said with a bit of disgust.

We noticed that the group ahead of us were slowing down and heading to a grove of trees. It looked like a wide lush spot with shade and protection. I was tired and my shoulders hurt and I was sure that Mary was equally, if not more, ready to call it a day.

We fell into the same routine as the previous two nights. I unpacked the donkey and brought the pack to Mary. She prepared our light dinner, and we enjoyed our solace and God's night show.

17

MARY

We awoke to what we hoped would be the last day. The sky to the east did not look the least bit favorable for travel. Dark angry clouds were gathering and the wind was picking up. 'Before the rain comes the wind.' Joseph brought out two large pieces of leather he had borrowed from Nebet in case it rained. They each had been wrapped around two sticks. Joseph had to show me how this new idea from Nebet was suppose to work. The two sticks were to be held in one hand with one stick going to the left and the other to the right so it formed a V shape. The sheet of leather had two small holes about three feet apart towards the front of the sheet. We were to raise the sheet over our head with the sticks to resemble a tent so that we could shield our heads and deflect the rain. Brilliant idea! We assembled the contraption to have it ready in case it began to rain.

It did.

Buckets.

Cats and dogs. I never did understand that phrase.

Big thick fat drops of rain.

At first I was angry with God for letting this happen. He was in control of the weather. Couldn't He make it sunny the entire trip?

The heavy rain bounced up from the ground and it soaked our feet and garments all the way up to our knees. It instantly made the clothing heavy and burdensome.

I could begin to feel the anger inside of me warming my skin. But I quickly pushed that notion away and took every thought captive.

"Dear God, show me the good part of this."

Well, the rain was warm.

The wind had ceased.

There was no thunder or lightning to worry about.

The donkey did not seem to mind.

Joseph did not seem to mind.

The road was flat and not too muddy.

The rain made the snakes hide.

"Okay, Thanks, God. Got it."

My new sunny disposition broke through the dark clouds of my mind.

I reached between my legs and grabbed the back of my long robe from behind and pulled it forward and up and girded it in my belt.

Joseph looked at me with quizzical eyes.

"You men do it to make your work easier. Why can't I?"

It really makes walking less cumbersome, too; I guess men do know a thing or two.

We walked in the rain for most of the day. We knew Jerusalem was near and then Bethlehem lay directly south. The journey was coming to an end.

"Thank You, God, that I have made it this far without any complications."

I may have spoken too soon.

About the ninth hour of the day the foremen began to motion us to take cover in a natural alcove. We were too far from the front of the caravan to see what was going on. We obeyed dutifully and did not ask any questions. We still had several hours of daylight left in which to travel and I just knew in my heart we could make it to Bethlehem tonight.

Maybe that was more wishful thinking than any reality based

on facts.

Frankly, I was not sure how much more I could take. I was trying very hard not to show Joseph my discomfort. A couple of times when I felt sharp pains in my abdomen, I was able to cover up the pain by pretending to misstep on the path. I don't know if Joseph was buying it but there was no sense in both of us worrying.

Joseph turned to me and said, "I'm going to go up to the next group and see if Eli knows anything. Perhaps I can get a better look as to why we are stopping and appear to be hiding."

I nodded my head and found a large boulder to sit upon and rest. I tried not to look at my feet. I knew they would be swollen beyond recognition.

I looked up towards the Jordan to my left and then to my right and up towards the western sky. The rain was easing up and I could see the clouds breaking up in the distance. I leaned back against the rocky cave like bunker and shut my eyes. I was instantly asleep and dreaming.

I was home with Mama and Abba and the children sitting around the table eating. It was always loud with laughter and conversation at our dinner table. Abba was not like most men who believed children should be seen and not heard. He encouraged us to engage in conversation and welcomed questions and a little silliness from the younger kids. Someone always had a guessing game and the winner got the last piece of bread.

I dreamed I was eating the last piece, the end piece, and my favorite. It was still warm, and it made the slice of cheese that I had wrapped in it melt. Abba had surprised us that evening with a skin of goat's milk. I was washing down the warm bread and cheese with some milk and just about to swallow when I felt someone shaking my shoulder.

"Mary. Mary. We can continue now."

I thought, NO NO, I want to eat this bread!!

Drats. I'm back sitting on the hard rock soaking wet and hungry.

Reality can really stink sometimes.

"Okay Joseph."

I laid my palms on the boulder and with all my energy I hoisted my backside off the rock.

OYE VAY!! Why do women keep doing this? I can see being misled into having one child, but to do it over and over women must have incredibly short memories.

I faked a smile and said, "Lead the way, my prince."

"The foremen had seen a band of marauders up ahead," Joseph informed me. "They thought it would be best to hide and let them continue east."

It had been their experience that a small band would challenge a larger group like ours and attempt a raid. So they decided to lay low and not take any risks. They asked if we were all wiling to pick up the pace and we could make Bethlehem shortly after dark.

I inhaled deeply and slowly let out my breath. "Bring it on. Let's do this."

The rain had stopped.

The next two hours passed without incident or much conversation.

We began to break upon a ridge, and there she was.

Bethlehem. How still we see thee lie.

Just behind the small city was the setting sun. It was like a bright orange welcome banner across the sky. Busting at the seams of the earth was a bright crimson ball pushing its way to the other side of the earth to wake them up.

The finish line was within reach. We quickened our pace. Well, we hastened as much a woman in my state could make haste and made it to the gate of Bethlehem in the dark.

The caravan had arrived ahead of us and dispersed to find their own accommodations.

Joseph and I walked with the donkey to the market place in the middle of the town. Even though it was well past sunset, the peddlers were still selling their wares.

"We have a little bit of money, would you like something to eat, Mary?" Joseph asked.

"If we could afford it, I sure would like something sweet and juicy.   Do you think we can find some grapes or pomegranates?

"You sit here and let me see what I can find," Joseph offered.

"You don't have to tell me twice. I will be glad to sit and wait." I lowered myself on a bench next to the town's well.

Joseph leaned close to me and gently held my chin with his fingertips. Holding my eyes with his he said, "I will be back as soon as I can. You are a real trouper, Mary. Thank you for being such a good sport. I know this whole thing has not been easy for you. I never thought saying yes to God would be so difficult, but we should have known better. We have read scripture to know that the men God chooses to do His will never have an easy time of it. But the pain is worth the glory of being a chosen vessel of God Almighty."

"Thank you, Joseph. But you must not have noticed when I was having a melt down," I said through a thin smile. "God never gives us more than we can handle. He promised to be with us. That is the one thing I remember the angel saying. It is what keeps me going every day."

"I love you, Mary."

"I love you too, Joseph. Now be a good betrothed husband and go get me some food," I said playfully.

"Yes ,my lady! At your service" he returned with good humor and mimicking a low bow and a full sweep of his arm.

I watched him walk towards the vendors. He left me to tend to the donkey and the pack. I hoped the donkey would not relieve himself and make a mess that I would have to clean up.

I looked at the new surroundings. With Bethlehem in close proximity to Jerusalem it was becoming very cosmopolitan. It had street torches and a planned out city structure. The streets were wide, and the new construction had a very pronounced Roman flavor. I let my gaze fall on the passersby. Some looked merry and entertained. Some pockets of people seemed to be in a festive mood. Others were as far from celebratory as they could be. They were worn and beaten down. I could not tell the natives from the visitors.

Joseph returned with a small cluster of grapes and a fresh supply of water.

"I inquired of an inn and a place to secure the donkey. A few people told me there were three inns in town. Let's eat these grapes and then call it a night. Tomorrow we can register with the census and then see what happens," he informed me.

"Sure, that sounds great." I was ravenous and tried to restrain myself from shoving all the grapes in my mouth at once. I had to remind myself that I was a lady and not a tomboy anymore. My brothers and I used to see how many grapes we could fit in our mouths and still breathe. I was the reigning queen and held the household record at 33. This was not the time to show Joseph my hidden talent.

Like an unexpected sting from a bee, I felt a sharp pain in my abdomen. It stole my breath.

"UHHH." I groaned.

I grabbed my belly which I had learned to use as a make-shift table, as the grapes rolled off. It felt peculiarly hard like a boulder.

Joseph froze. He had no idea what to say, what to do, what to think. I think he was afraid to touch me as well. He just sat and gazed at me, his mouth a gap.

I tried to exhale and breathe deeply to relax. The initial sharp pain began to turned dull, and within a few minutes my abdomen relinquished its hardened state and returned to normal.

I opened my eyes as I allowed my shoulders and neck to relax, and I tried to return to rhythmic breathing.

Joseph and I stared at each other. How can we be prepared and not have a clue what to do at the same time?

"I think we might have a little visitor soon." I said with some comic relief.

"Are you alright?" Joseph finally found his voice.

"Yes, I am. Mama told me that the pain would start slowly and then build gradually. She told me when I start to feel pain and my belly starts to harden and then soften that I should find a midwife."

"Are you able to walk?" Joseph stood up and was looking around for something.

"The pain has passed and I feel fine now." I was speaking the truth much to my surprise.

"Let's go find those inns," Joseph said as he reached for my hand to help me to my feet.

I struck the pose that has become all too familiar and comfortable- my hands on my lower back and my chest extended. My lungs felt like they were being forced into a small box. I took inventory of my body and was astonished to find that I was free of pain and had a resurgence of energy.

"Let's walk quickly while I still feel fine," I suggested and reached down for the reins of the donkey. I handed them to Joseph, and we began to head north on the torch-lit street.

It was getting late, and there were many people still on the streets. We knocked on the door of the first innkeeper. We did not think he would have retired for the evening yet. A small thin man leaning on a cane opened the door slightly. He eyed us with distrustful suspicion. "Whaddaya want!" he snarled.

"Have you any room available?" Joseph used his extra polite voice to show the innkeeper we were civil, well-mannered people.

"NO! I'm full." And he slammed the door.

We stood there stunned.

"There are two other inns, Joseph," I said, trying to keep my voice steady after such a verbal assault. "Let's walk down the street.

Two blocks over we knocked on the second door. This time a kindly woman who resembled my Mama opened the door. She smiled at Joseph and then at me, and I followed her eyes to my bulging belly.

"Oh my, you look like you are ready to have that baby any time now, dear."

"Yes, ma'am, I started to feel pain just a few minutes ago. We need to find a midwife and a place to stay," I quickly interjected trying to step into the open arms of her good graces.

The kind lady took a step inside her house and called,"Esther!" A young girl not much younger than I came swiftly to her side. "Get your brother Simeon and make haste to find Abijah the midwife. Tell her we are in need of her tonight." Within minutes Esther and an older boy pushed past us and disappeared into the night as Esther swiftly tied her scarf over her dark curly hair.

"Thank you very much," said Joseph.

"Not at all dear. Have you been married very long?" she asked, not knowing that Joseph and I were not legally married yet but merely as a means of ascertaining if we were trustworthy enough to be welcomed into her inn.

"As a matter of fact, ma'am, we have not been married yet...you see..."

It was as if someone stuck a tube in the woman's navel and began to blow air into her. Her chest rose, her shoulders became more erect, her eyes bulged and her eyebrows seemed as if they would touch her hairline. She sucked in air and stared at us as she held her breath. She looked down at us over her nose and raised her chin.

"WELL, I NEVER! THERE IS ABSOLUTLEY NO POSSIBLE WAY I CAN ALLOW THE LIKES OF YOU TWO TO STAY AT MY INN. I HAVE A REPUTATION TO UPHOLD!"

I had never seen anyone change character as quickly as I had seen her change. The wind that accompanied the slamming of the door actually made my veil billow.

Whether it was the shock of the emotional brutality or an actual contraction, I grabbed Joseph's arm and doubled over in pain. The hardness of my belly returned, and I breathed in and out as slowly as I could to keep myself calm until it was over. These episodes only lasted a few minutes, but it sure seemed like eternity.

Again, within a few minutes my belly softened and returned to 'normal.'

It really was not pain as much as it was discomfort like I was trying to hold up a huge rock with my thighs.

I regained my composure, and we went to find the last of the Bethlehem inns.

We were walking to the other end of town when Esther and

her brother walked by with a woman in tow. Esther pointed to me, left the woman standing near us and continued home. The woman looked at me, and then her eyes dropped to my belly.

"Shalom. My name is Abijah. Have you had much pain yet?" she said as she reached out to lay her knowing hand on my abdomen.

"Yes, sharp pains come quickly and radiate down my legs. My abdomen gets really hard for several minutes and then relaxes," I informed Abijah.

There was something really familiar about her. Her face was veiled, of course, but her eyes held familiarity.

"Where are you staying tonight?" Abijah asked.

Joseph interjected, "We have not found a place yet but we have one last inn to try."

"When you find a place make sure you have clean blankets and sheets and then send someone for me. I have a home next to the old baker's place. It is easy to find. Everyone knows me."

Joseph and I nodded in unison. The magnitude of the situation was beginning to find a home on our shoulders.

"You will be just fine," Abijah said as if reading our minds. "I do this everyday, and God will be with you. He created this you know." She winked at me, and I could tell she was smiling under her veil. "I will be ready any time you send for me. Don't be concerned with the hour of the night. Babies don't know the time of day. They come when they want. I believe your little blessing will come tonight." With another wink she left us.

"I feel better about this." I said to reassure Joseph. "She seems very capable and there is something familiar about her, I can't quite place her. There is no way I would know her."

Wordlessly, Joseph turned to walk up the street on his left and began to lead us in a daze.

I was glad he could not see me smile under my veil at his bewilderment.

Child bearing always bamboozles men. It is one area in which they are completely disoriented and are totally out of their   control.

154

LUKE 2:6-7 WHILE THEY WERE THERE, THE TIME CAME FOR THE BABY TO BE BORN AND SHE GAVE BIRTH TO HER FIRST BORN, A SON. SHE WRAPPED HIM IN CLOTHS AND PLACED HIM IN A MANGER, BECAUSE THERE WAS NO ROOM FOR THEM IN THE INN.

18

JOSEPH

I worried about Mary. The pain seemed to come more quickly now. If she were not overly afraid, then I should not be either. Hannah seemed to have prepared her for some of the experience, but still. So much could go wrong. *'God is my salvation, I will trust and not be afraid, He is my strength'* (Isaiah 12:2). I kept repeating that to myself as I walked up the last street to the last inn. What if we cannot find a place to stay? Can we stay in the town square? What if Mary has that baby tonight? We can't have that baby in the open air? Listen to me, I said 'we' as if I were going to do it with her. "Help me trust in Thee God. I don't think I am doing a very good job of it. Dear God, please let there be room at the next inn." I guess I was pleading with God more than asking. After all it was His Son, He would not have him born outside. "Thank You that You sent Abijah."

We wound up the hill to the last inn. Mary sat on a bench outside the door of the inn. I gave her the reins of the donkey, and I knocked on the door. It was getting late and I prayed we were not disturbing or waking the keepers. I knocked again, getting nervous that the hour was too late to do business.

The door slowly opened, and a large man filled the doorway. "May I help you?" he said in a deep booming voice. I would have taken him for a farmer or blacksmith instead of an innkeeper.

"Please, sir, my wife is feeling birthing pains. Have you a room available?" Joseph said in a voice draped with desperation.

The keeper's voice and body size did not match the compassion in his eyes. He looked outside the door and down at Mary sitting on the bench against the wall and holding the reins of the beast. Her eyes were closed and her hand was gently resting on her swollen belly. His gaze returned to me. He shook his head slowly. "I am so sorry young man, I just gave up the last room for the night. There are two other inns in town." He offered.

"Thanks just the same," said Joseph in defeat. "They are

full also."

"Come on, Mary." I turned away from the large man standing in the open door and reached for Mary's hand to help her stand. We began to retrace our steps side by side, followed by the clip clap echoes of the donkey's hooves.

Rejection, dejection, depression, despair and all their family members began to take up residence in my heart and head.

I actually felt a tear form in my eye. I did not have the strength to raise my hand and brush it away. I was an utter failure. I could not even secure a place for my pregnant wife to deliver our, God's, child. What was God thinking? You would think the Master of the universe, the Most High God would find a man who was capable of taking care of His Son. If I cannot do something as simple as finding an appropriate place for Jesus to be born how the heck was I going to provide for and raise His Son?

A second tear welled up. My throat began to tighten.

I have not cried since Mother's death. I could not imagine that I would ever experience grief of that magnitude again. I was wrong. So very wrong.

I was beginning to let the sledge hammer of hopelessness beat me on the anvil of our circumstances.

As the third tear followed the leader down my cheek, I heard the innkeeper say, "Wait up, son."

I quickly wiped at my eyes and turned to face him. We were only a few yards away. My entire pity party had taken place in a matter of a few steps.

"I have a large barn in the back," the man motioned over his shoulder. "I have offered it to other people, so I don't know exactly how many have taken me up on my offer but you can stay there for free. I have my animals and those of my guests tied up in there also, but it is warm with sturdy walls and I just unloaded a bunch of clean, fresh straw in there. It is not much but it is all I can offer."

I looked at Mary for her opinion.

"Let's go take a look," Mary said. "At least we can rest there until something else comes up."

"Thank you, sir." I said to the keeper, and we started to turn around and move in the direction to which he had pointed.

We made our way to the backside of the inn. Sure enough there was a three-sided pole barn with the open end facing the south. It did look sturdy, I'll grant him that. As we approached, we became aware that indeed many people were at a loss for proper shelter as well. We wandered in the open side and surveyed our surroundings. The barn had four major sections. The innkeeper and his guests' animals were corralled in the northwest corner. I counted six people seeking refuge. Looking around I saw one open stall that was unoccupied by man or beast. I motioned for Mary to claim the stall for our own and led the donkey to join the company of the other beasts. I relieved the animal of our pack and carried it back to Mary. I flattened the straw and found that it was, to be sure, free from any residue from previous inhabitants. The smell of animal dung was coming from places other than our corner of the world. It looked as if this was the area where the keeper kept his supply of fresh hay to distribute through out the barn.

I pulled our two blankets out of our pack and handed them to Mary who laid them out flat. I noticed that she was having another pain. What did Abijah call it? A contraction? She was standing up, leaning her left hand on the wall and rocking back and forth. Her breathing was deep but even and controlled. With her eyes shut, I watched her rock in a rhythm with her pain. Deep breath, rock forward, exhale, rock back, inhale deeply, rock forward, exhale, rock backward. Her right hand was on her back as if to keep it from breaking in two from the weight of her belly. This dance went on for several minutes. I knew it was over when I heard Mary exhale a long controlled breath and stand up straight. She rolled her shoulders back and looked my way to see if I had been aware of her discomfort. She smiled weakly at me.

"We will get through this Mary. God promised He would be with us. I believe he sent Abijah to us." I tried to reassure Mary as I helped her to find comfort on the blankets.

"Elizabeth!" Mary shouted. "That is from where I remember Abijah! She helped Elizabeth deliver John! She was terrific. I cannot believe she is here in Bethlehem! Did God send her here to help us, too?"

"God works in mysterious ways. Nothing surprises me anymore," I responded to Mary in a lighthearted manner.

"God is good all the time." Mary said.

"And all the time, God is good." I echoed back.

"Do you want me to go find her and bring her to you now?" I asked Mary.

"No, not just yet. Mamma said that the first baby takes a while to come. The baby lives in a sack of water in my belly. The baby breaks that sack of water when it is ready.

She said when the water breaks, then the time for delivery comes closer and faster. I suggest we wait till that happens. When I was with Elizabeth she had these contractions for several hours before John was born. So I do not think it will be anytime soon." Mary spoke with a clear head as if the birth was going to happen to someone else.

"I'll get the rest of those grapes, and we will just settle in then, okay?" It was all I was able to offer her for solace. I felt incredibly inept.

"Dear God," I prayed. "I cannot believe there is no room for us at any proper inns. I cannot believe we are staying in a filthy barn. I know all things work out for the good for those who love You and are called according to Your purpose. Well, we are definitely called according to Your purpose. Please show me some good things about this situation."

I glanced around the barn and out the open side that was facing south. It was a warm night. I began to find things worthy of praise.

Thank You that it is not cold and raining.

It was a clear night and full of stars. Thank You God that it is not going to rain and that You have Your spectacular night show to keep us entertained.

Thank You for the innkeeper who offered us his barn. I pray a special blessing upon him. Thank You that he had the means to buy new straw and that there was a place for us.

Thank You that we have enough food.

Thank You, God for always providing for us.

Thank You that we arrived safely.

Thank You for the foremen of the caravan who led us here safely.

Thank You for sending Abijah. What a coincidence that she helped Elizabeth and now she is here...or is it?

Thank You that Mary is not a whiner.

Thank You that You gave me a strong woman with a sturdy

constitution. She will teach Your Son well.

Please, God, help Mary through this delivery. Please be particularly benevolent and cause it to go as smoothly and pain-free as possible. She is so young. Please help her body to birth this baby without any complications.

Thank You for helping me take my eyes off the situation and turn them towards You and Your glory.

I was gazing out at the stars and was taking in the silvery quarter moon. I turned to Mary to point it out to her and found her sound asleep. She was actually snoring! What a woman! Sleeping while in labor.

I draped my cloak over her and slipped out of the barn to take in the surroundings while being careful to stay close and within earshot in case Mary should call for me. Several men were out on the street standing around and shooting the breeze. There are such few occasions for Israelites to meet fellow Jews from other tribes. The Jews have become so numerous and scattered throughout the land but we can always trace our heritage back to one of twelve tribes. Almost everyone here could be from the tribe of Judah in the line of King David. One man certainly produced quite a number of descendants. But not everyone in Bethlehem is here for the census. Some live here, some already traveled for the census in another town and made their way back to their home in Bethlehem. It did look like a pretty little town from what I could see in the dark. I can see why people would migrate here.

I came upon a small group of men in conversation. I chuckled to myself. No matter the town, the manly conversation are always the same; crops, weather, politics, taxes, Romans. Always careful not to say what one really thinks about the last three. Rome had many ears. They do not take kindly to treason. One man, who was tall and thin and looked like he was in much need of a wife who cooked, said he was experimenting with a new crop he had planted in the spring. The spring rains had been favorable and he anticipated a bumper harvest. Another man with broad shoulders and large hands with the distinct aroma of a sheep farmer said he had added a new breed of sheep to his herd that was to produce a special kind of wool that would repel water. His wife was a weaver, and they planned to make some sample blankets after the first sheering next week.

One man, who appeared more scholarly than laborer, turned to me and asked me where I was from.

"I am from up north in Galilee, in Nazareth to be exact. I came here to register for the census." I figured they probably already knew that. Bethlehem was not a vacationing hotspot.

"That must have been quite the trip." Slim commented.

"We traveled in a caravan of thirty other people. It took us four days but we had a great crew of guides who got us here without mishap." I wanted to make sure I gave the foremen the public credit that was due them.

Sheep sheering Sam said, "Did I see you coming out of Jake's barn? Are you staying there?"

"Yes, my wife and I could not find any room at the inns. The last innkeeper, you say his name is Jake, offered us the barn. We gratefully took it." I decided to call Mary my wife and not tell them the actual truth. I was dealing with enough of an internal ordeal, I did not need an external one also. I hope God does not mind my lie.

"You are welcome to join a few of us men out in the open field but it would not be proper for your wife," commented the sheep shearer. "I have been tending sheep most of my life, and I have probably spent as many nights under the stars as under a roof. I have three large flocks now out in the field being tended by my hired men."

I bet you have helped ewes deliver your share of sheep too," I remarked more as an inside joke than an actual fact.

"More than I can count. It is the MOST natural instinct in the world. A female body just knows what to do and lets nature take its course. I am only speaking of sheep, ya know. When my wife was having our 6 kids, I was at the pub yukking it up with the other men. I wasn't going anywhere near my house! Sheep bleating in pain I can tolerate, women...I don't think so," SS Sam said laughing as he shook his head.

Mr. Scholar laughed, "It is no place for a man when a woman is giving birth. God did not make men to help. That is women's work. Our work was done nine months ago." He threw his head back and howled at his own joke. The others joined in what they thought was uproarious hilarity and elbowed each other as they recalled their private escapades.

How did this conversation take this turn? My wife lay within twenty feet of us on the verge of a virgin birth and these men were laughing about the tryst they had to get their women to this state! It was all too surreal!

They were still laughing at their memories and Mr. Scholar's joke when I bid them a good evening and excused myself and made my way back to the barn.

Geesh. Did I feel better or worse? SS Sam did make a comforting comment-"It was the most natural thing in the world."

I sure hope so.

I bid the men a good night, and went back to Mary. She was still snoring in her sweet young female way. Finding my place next to her I was staring at the ceiling and marveling at the circumstances in the past nine months that have brought me to be in a barn in Bethlehem.

My eyelids grew heavy and I allowed my body to be absorbed into the straw and followed Mary's breathing pattern into my own deep dreams.

19

MARY

"My heart rejoices in the LORD; in the LORD my strength is lifted high. There is no one holy like the LORD; there is no one besides you; there is no Rock like our God." (1Samuel 2:1-2) Those words were familiar words. All Jewish girls learned the song of Hannah from the scriptures. She prayed for years for a baby and the LORD finally answered her. She named the baby Samuel and he became a great judge of Israel. These words, this song, was going through my head as something awakened me. I opened one eye. The smell of straw, hay and animal dung was becoming overwhelming. I wish I could say that it took me a few minutes to remember where I was. No such luck. I opened the other eye and looked around. Joseph was sound asleep lying next to me. He had put his cloak over me to stay warm. What a guy. He was always sacrificing for others.

What had awakened me? My back was aching but that did not surprise me. I had, after all, slept in a barn on straw. Yup, I had back pain. It was a constant throbbing in my lower back. I leaned up on my elbows. No relief. I rolled on my left side and brought my right leg up. No relief. I rolled on my right side. No relief. Now that I was awake, I might as well go find a facility. I rolled on my left and got to my hands and knees. I crawled the short distance to the wall and braced my hand against it to steady myself while I got my legs under me. What an ordeal. I cannot believe it has taken me three minutes to stand up. I used to outrun boys and climb trees and jump over creeks! Now I cannot even stand up without support. Why would a woman ever do this more than once? I will NEVER do this again. I must be crazy to do this in the first place.

I got to my feet and leaned against the stall wall to get my balance. I put both hands on my lower back looking for a little relief. No change. With my right hand against the wall for support, I bent backwards to try and stretch.

Suddenly GUSH!

OH MY HEAVENS! WHAT IS THAT?! AM I WETTING MYSELF?

I tried to suppress my fright and clamped my hand over my mouth. I knew what this was. Mama had tried to explain it.

But it was still terrifying. I'm glad I was already leaning against the wall for support. Now the wall was responsible to bear my total weight. And believe you me, it was substantial weight!

I leaned and waited for the water to stop flowing. I tried to get my robe out of the way without much success.

What should I do?

"Joseph...Joseph," I briskly whispered. I knew there were others in the barn and it had to be late in the night. The animals were very still and so were the people. I could even hear some of them snoring.

"JOSEPH!"

I reached out my foot to try and touch him but I was too far away or I was too short however you wanted to look at it.

I huffed out in exasperation.

"JOSEPH!" I whispered a little louder. I was rapidly beginning not to care if I awoke the fellow barn mates.

No response.

I took one step forward and then another with my feet wide apart so as not to get my robe any more wet than I already had.

I was standing next to Joseph and he was lying on his left side facing away from me.

"JOSEPH." I said a little more insistently. I lay my right foot on his shoulder and gave him a healthy nudge.

So there I was. Standing in a very vulnerable position. My left foot was on uneven ground covered in straw with my left hand supporting my lower back and my right foot resting on Joseph's shoulder and my right hand out to the side for balance.

"Joseph!" This time with a bit of force in my voice. He rolled over and my foot rolled with him! His movement knocked me off balance and I swung to my right as I grabbed at the air for a handhold. I did not find one.

"AHHH" WHAM! I fell on my right side landing on the only mound of straw that had not been distributed yet. It had absorbed my weight and kept me from hitting the hard ground. Thank You, God.

Joseph shot up like a slingshot and was standing with outstretched arms.

"Mary, oh Mary! Are you all right?" Utter panic filled his voice. "I am so sorry. What had I done?

I lay still for a few moments making a mental assessment of my faculties. I felt no pain in my abdomen or my back. I was okay.

Joseph bent down and wrapped his strong arms all the way around me and hoisted me to my feet. He quickly began to brush the straw off my clothing and out of my hair.

"Mary, are you all right? Why are you awake?" His voice was husky with sleep.

"I think you should go find Abijah, she said not to be concerned with the time of day or night. She said babies always seemed to want to come in the middle of the night." Again, my attempt at comic relief.

"Tell her my water has broken. She will know what that means."

Joseph led me back to our blankets. He reshaped the two smaller ones and tried to pile up the straw against the back wall for a little padded support for me.

"I'll be back as soon as I can," he reassured me as he fled in haste.

"Hurry!" I called to his back.

Alone.

But not really.

I had the Creator of the heavens and the earth, God Almighty, the Most High God, Jehovah Jireh, the God who provides, with me here in this stinking barn.

"God will be with you," the angel had promised me.

Okay God. It is time. I cannot believe I have failed You, and I am giving birth to Your Son in a barn full of strangers and smelly animals. You deserve better than this. I should be in a nice warm bed with clean sheets and my...and my ... my Mama her to help me!

I started to cry. My throat tightened as it squeezed the tears up and out of my eyes and overflowed down my cheeks. I didn't know if I was crying for me because I was so scared or crying because the Son of God was going to be born in such a lowly state.

"MAMA! I sobbed. "I want my Mama!"

Then I saw a glow. I presumed it was a torch being carried by Abijah and Joseph. I quickly realized the glow was much too bright and intense for a torch. The scene mesmerized me. I felt tremendous warmth and comfort from the radiance.

"Mary. Favored one. Do not be afraid. I AM here." The voice came from the blaze.

And it vanished.

Just as quickly as it had appeared, it disappeared.

Shell-shocked, I held my breath mid-sob. I sniffed my nose, swallowed the sob and wiped my tears. I sat in the afterglow and let the words of comfort fall upon me.

I closed my eyes and sniffed my nose again.

I inhaled deeply, held it for a few moments, and exhaled slowly and with control.

With my eyes closed I could still see the after glow of the bright light in the corner of the barn. I began to feel tingly all over, from my toes, my ankles, my calves, up to my legs and back and belly and chest and neck, all the way to the follicles of my hair. God was warming every inch of my body.

He created birth. He designed the woman's body to do this. He will be with me.

Blessed is the man whose trust is in the LORD and whose hope is the LORD

I said it out loud.

"Blessed is the man whose trust is in the LORD and whose hope is the LORD."

Again. Louder!

"Blessed is the man whose trust is in the LORD and whose hope is the LORD." (Jeremiah 17:7)

That's when I felt the first intense pain. It was as if someone pierced my side with a sharp rod.

"AHHH!" I groaned such a primal sound that it frightened me.

176

I rolled to my left side to try to escape the pain.

"AAUGH!" Again the sound of a wounded animal left my lips.

Within a minute the pain subsided.

I lay back and tried to steady my breathing.

Where was Joseph? Where is Abijah?

I managed to get my breathing under control.

I heard some pounding on the flattened earth outside the barn. Joseph rushed in with his face flushed. He was carrying some blankets. He dropped them at my feet and rushed to my side. Kneeing in the straw he began to stroke my hair. "I'm here, Mary. Everything will be all right."

Abijah was two steps behind him and had a young girl at her side. They were both remarkably calm which instantly eased my anxious heart.

"Hello, Mary." Abijah said in a voice as calm and serene as

the velvet night sky. "How are you feeling? Has the pain begun to get worse?"

"Yes. I have had two really sharp pains. My Mama told me to try and control my breathing and it will help keep me calm."

"Your mother is a very wise woman. She is exactly right. When the pain comes, try to see the baby in your mind moving down the birth canal. Think of your breath as cushioning her along the way," Abijah counseled me in her calm melodious voice. "This is Leah, my assistant. Leah, this is Mary from Nazareth."

"Nice to make your acquaintance," Leah said in a small girlish voice. "You are in very good hands. Abijah is the very best. She feels her work is ordained by God," Leah added with a knowing smile.

"Thank you for helping me."

Leah just nodded and began to do her part of the work. She had produced a rope from under her stack of blankets and strung it across the beams of our little stall. She then draped two lightweight blankets over it to make a partition and provide us with some privacy.

178

Abijah turned to Joseph. He looked up at her with terror in his tear-filled eyes. She seemed to be conveying some message to him without using words. I followed the invisible line of communication between the two of them. I looked at Joseph and then up at Abijah and then back to Joseph. Joseph looked quizzically at her. He had no idea what she was trying to say.

"Joseph. It is time for you to leave." She said very matter-of-factly. It left no room for discussion. It was a statement, not a request.

As Joseph leaned on his elbow to begin to stand, another pain rolled over me like a stampede of cattle.

"AAHHHH!" My head was thrown back in agony and my spine arched to fend off the onslaught of pain.

"Breathe Mary," Abijah's words floated down to me on clouds of down feathers. No hint of anxiety or distress. Just calm soothing words. Then she began to lead me in a rhythmic breathing pattern.

"Big inhale, Mary, then exhale slowly." She breathed with me to demonstrate.

"Again. Big inhale and slowly exhale all the air."

We breathed in unison. I glanced sideways at Joseph who was following us with his own breathing. I caught the scent of his breath. It made me chuckle on the inside. If only his friends could see him breathing like some old lady in labor.

"One last time, dear. Good. Do you feel better? Has the contraction subsided?"

I opened my eyes as the last exhale was exhausted.

"Okay, that was not so bad." I said in truth.

"Ah hum." Abijah cleared her throat.

Both Joseph and I looked up at her.

She looked at Joseph and threw her head towards the opening of the barn-her signal for him to high tail it out of there.

"OH...yeah... right." He stammered and leaned over to kiss my sweaty forehead. He righted himself and brushed the straw clinging to his robe.

"I'll be right outside if you need me."

Leah handed Joseph two pitchers. "Please go fill these with warm water and leave them by the door. Hurry!"

Joseph took the pitchers without a word, nodded affirmation to Leah and left.

You know the only thing I thought at that very moment? It took him not even two seconds to go from lying next to me fully reclined and propped on one elbow to a full straight back stance, and it had taken me three minutes to achieve the same just moments earlier.

Where is the justice?

My pity party was rudely interrupted with another sharp pain.

The pains were swiftly becoming more powerful and were trying to make a child out of me.

Leah had taken the place of Joseph at my side and was breathing with me.

Big inhale.

Slow, controlled exhale.

Big inhale.

Slow, controlled exhale.

I let out another guttural moan.

Last controlled exhale.

I lay back on the straw.

Exhausted.

I was really sweating. I have not sweat this much since before I met Joseph. My two younger brothers and I would race to the creek and see who could jump over without getting their feet wet. We were always having contests. No chore was done without a friendly wager as who could…

"AAHHHH." My throat felt like a gravel pit. It was so dry with the heavy breathing and rough with the grunting.

"Okay, Mary. We are almost finished." Abijah coached me on.

Big inhale.

Slow, controlled exhale.

Big inhale.

"Okay stop." Abijah commanded. "Let me unwrap the umbilical cord that is wound around his neck, and it will be all over.

Leah puckered her lips and puffed like she was blowing out a candle.

"Do like this Mary." Leah demonstrated.

I dutifully obeyed.

Puff, puff, puff, puff.

"Okay Mary, one last big breath!" Abijah sounded as excited as if it were her child.

"It's a... it's a... it's a boy!"

And with those words the sound I had been waiting to hear for nine long months filled the barn!

Leah was kneeling next to Abijah now with a clean white cloth. Abijah gently lay the crying Jesus in her waiting hands and she briskly but gently cleaned him off. "Hello, sweety pie. Welcome to Bethlehem. Now don't cry, darling, I'm working as fast as I can to get you clean and dry and warm. I'll get you to your mama in just a minute."

The tenderness with which Leah spoke to Jesus was a memory I will cherish forever. If she only knew to Whom she was speaking. I wish I could tell her. She would never believe me. I hope she believes God.

Leah held Jesus firmly as Abijah took a small sharp knife and cut the umbilical cord and tied it off with a small bit of string. She then relieved Leah of the baby while Leah went to the door to retrieve the pitchers of water.

She brought a basin to Abijah and filled it with the warm water from one of the pitchers that Joseph had obediently left at the door. As Abijah laid Jesus on the hay she withdrew a small vial of oil from her apron pocket and emptied it into the water. Sweet fragrance filled the air and I was immediately transported back to the time with Elizabeth. It was the same frangrance Abijah used for John. She dipped a small clean cloth into the water and began to clean Jesus and speak soft cooing words to him. I watched as Jesus crunched his face as he cried. His little hands all balled up into fists and legs shaking in protest. There is no lovelier sound than an infant's cry. "Now, now, sweet boy, try to relax and enjoy your first bath," Abijah soothingly spoke to Jesus.

Leah then brought a second basin and knelt next to me. She poured the second pitcher of water into her basin and mixed it with her own vial of oil. A different but equally luscious aroma mingled with the first. She took her own cloth and began to wash my forehead and neck. I closed my eyes and allowed her to minister to me. It was the most extravagant pampering I had ever received. She washed my face, neck, shoulders and under my arms. I lay there almost trance like. Leah hummed softly as she lavished love on me.

Thank You, God were the only words that ran through my foggy brain.

I opened my eyes to watch Abijah tend to Jesus. With the grace and compassion of a fine artist, Abijah swaddled Jesus tightly in strips of cloth. She made one last effort to gingerly wipe at his face with the corner of the cloth to make him as perfectly clean as she could before she presented him to me.

He had calmed down by now and was making little grunting noises as he tried to adjust to His new world.

He was pink and perfect and round and...beautiful.

"Hello, my precious. Mama is here." I leaned forward to kiss his forehead. He felt so soft and smelled so delightful. "Do you feel all better now? Abijah did such a wonderful job cleaning you up, and you smell so good."

It is funny how a person automatically speaks to a baby in a high pitched sing-song voice. It comes as natural as swaying back and forth while holding a baby.

I loved being a mother already.

Thank You, God. You were indeed with me. Look at Your Son. Isn't He wonderful?

I had not noticed that Leah had snuck out to reclaim Joseph.

He rushed to our side and knelt down next to us.

"How are you feeling?" Joseph breathlessly asked.

"Better than I have felt in my entire life."

"You did a great job, honey." And he kissed my forehead. "You smell wonderful, too."

"Abijah was terrific." I looked up at her as she was packing her things.

"Thank you so much Abijah. I can't believe we found you here in Bethlehem."

"God works in mysterious ways," was her only reply with an added wink. "I'll come and check on you in the morning."

"Thank you." Joseph and I said in unison.

And she and Leah were gone. They left the hanging curtain for our privacy.

"Would you like to hold him?" I gestured to Joseph.

"Yes, but let me get something that I found while I was outside waiting." He quickly got up and left the barn.

This time I was not alone nor was I afraid. A heavenly peace washed over me and covered me like a fresh layer of fallen snow. I was totally and utterly in awe of what God had done for me and through me. I tried to let the moment sink in. I tried to etch every detail of this whole event in my memory. Knowing that if we have other children, (HA! Listen to me, a few hours ago I swore off more children), if we are blessed with more children, none would be like this.

Truly I thought my heart was going to burst. I could not contain the joy I was feeling right now. I think it did burst. The joy came rushing up out of my heart into my eyes and out of my face in the form of tears. Unabashedly I let them flow. I saw two tears drop on Jesus' face. I snickered and wiped them off with my sleeve. Then I wiped at my nose. Can't have that dropping on Jesus' face now, can we? I smiled at my joke. Always the jokester, aren't you Mary.

Joseph returned with an animal feeding trough. He set it next to me and then gathered some hay from the mound that earlier had braced my fall. He scooped up several armfuls and stuffed it into the trough. He reached for a small blanket that Abijah had left for us and laid it over the hay.

"I figured He would need a place to sleep. We can't be holding Him all the time, right?"

"That was a great idea, Joseph. Thank you for thinking so far in advance. I am ashamed to say it never crossed my mind."

"That is okay my dear," he said as he settled next to the baby and me, "You have been a little busy."

He mused as he reached out to hold Jesus who had long since stopped crying and was wide eyed taking in His surroundings.

"Now make sure you support his head," I instructed as I handed Him off to Joseph.

"Hey, little fella. How ya doing?" Even Joseph adopted the unconscious high-pitched baby talk.

Joseph stroked Jesus' cheek with his rough weathered forefinger. Jesus' eyes were riveted on Joseph as if understanding every word. Joseph stared back for a long time without uttering another sound. His face took on a visible change. It morphed from a euphoric new father to one of tremendous seriousness and trepidation.

"Do you know Who You are?" He spoke to Jesus slowly. "Do You know why You are here?"

And then a tear escaped from Joseph's eye and rolled down his cheek.

"Will You accept me as Your father?"

My own tears mirrored Joseph's.

What do we do now?

KING HEROD

MATTHEW 2:1-8 "DURING THE TIME OF KING HEROD, MAGI FROM THE EAST CAME TO JERUSALEM AND ASKED, 'WHERE IS THE ONE WHO HAS BEEN BORN KING OF THE JEWS?' WHEN KING HEROD HEARD THIS HE WAS DISTURBED.'"

20

KING HEROD

I did not sleep a wink. The wind was howling all night and the rain was dripping down one of the corners of my room. I got so cold I called the houseboy to add firewood to the fire and then it would get too hot. Blasted anyhow! Can't he get anything right? Too cold, then too hot. When I get through with him he will have wished he had never been my servant!

Sleep was elusive so I got up. Dawn was breaking, and it promised to be a miserable day. It should not be this cold yet. It was not the season! The cold bitter morning matched my mood perfectly. I yelled for my servants to bring me more robes. Blast them all!! Can't anyone get anything right!

Four housemen ran in bringing robes and slippers. Another stoked the fire and brought it back to life and tossed on two more logs. I sat with a thud onto my throne. I moved around trying to get comfortable with all these clothes on. I sat and admired my hands-perfectly manicured hands with a ring on each finger. I sneered to think that just one ring was worth more than most of these peasants in Judea made in a whole year. Filthy scoundrels, that's what they were! I ruled over a bunch of filthy scoundrels!

They never had it so good. I have built Judea into a showplace. I have built roads, gardens and magnificent buildings. For god's sake, I built them their temple! Truly a masterpiece of a structure! You would think those varmints would love me for that alone! I have made Jerusalem what it is today and they should fall on their knees and thank me.

Not only was the cold and wind keeping me awake but also I couldn't stop thinking about those heathens from the east. Kings, magi, astronomers! HA! Those savages, what do they know?! They paraded into town with their entourage like they were some gift from the gods. They asked to see me but I made them wait. I would not give them the satisfaction that they could command my attention just by showing up! I am a busy man! I am King of Judea! King of the Jews! They had to wait.

After I was good and ready, I had them ushered into the throne room. I wanted them to see my magnificent throne! I had robed myself in my finest robes and jewels and sat on my throne to receive them.

I hope no one saw the expression on my face when I saw the men stroll into the room. My mouth dropped open and I quickly snapped it shut. I did not give them the satisfaction of upstaging me. Their grandeur was astounding. I felt like sagebrush compared to their stateliness. They were so tall and dark-skinned. The fabric of their robes was like nothing I had ever seen; it almost glistened in the reflection of the flames of the fireplace. I could see from a distance that gold was woven into the cloth.

I instantly grew angry by how small I felt in their presence. I hated that feeling. I remembered all too well as a child the feelings of complete inferiority that plagued me. One never fully out grows that. No matter to what level one rises as an adult, that inferior little child lives embedded in one's souls. My inner child climbed out of the dungeon of my past to which I had relegated it and began whispering in my ear. "You little man, you are no match for these magi. Not only are they superior to your kingdom, but also they are superior to you intellectually. You are not worthy to untie their sandals."

The all too-familiar-anger started to boil in my bowels and began to rise up to my chest.

Like a well seasoned centurion, I had trained myself to control it and I was a master of disguising and commanding my true feelings.

I stood up.

"Gentlemen! Welcome," I said in a dramatic voice dripping with sarcasm. "My humblest apologies for keeping you waiting all day. My kingdom is vast and requires all my attention to keep things running smoothly. Let me offer you some refreshments. I am sure you are in need of something to take the chill out of your bones."

"Akbar!" I yelled, perhaps a bit too harshly. I'm good at charades but sometimes my anger get the best of me. "Akbar, bring nourishment."

I turned back to my guests, "To what do I owe the honor of this visit?"

It never crossed my mind that these heathens did not speak my language. I noticed one man stepped forward and stood between the entourage and me. He turned to the Persians and spoke something.

He then turned to me and said. "Shalom, me naam is Shakara. My maasta wish to know where iz de one who has been boorn keeng of da Jews?"

"What?" My mind was racing as I continued with my acting skills to hide my rage. "I have not seen nor heard of any baby born king of the Jews."

The interpreter turned to the magi to give my reply. Even I could understand a shoulder shrug and upturned palms. The universal language of "I dunno."

One of the magi spoke something and the interpreter said to me, " we haav been told lung ago dat one day a mighty keeng shull be boorn an shull rule his peepul with peace. Dat he will be culled da 'Prince uf peace an dat hees kingdom will reign foorever."

"Let me call in some of our holy men and chief priests and see what they have to say." I felt agitation rising in my chest.

The interpreter relayed the message.

"AKBAR!" I yelled. Dog gonnit, where was that boy!

Just then Akbar came in, followed by three

housemaids carrying trays of drinks and food. They set them on the side table and motioned for the magi to partake. Then the maids shuffled backwards towards the door, never daring to turn their back to the king.

"Akbar, go fetch the chief priest and teachers of the law. NOW!" My anger slipped out.

As we waited, we shared uncomfortable silence. Not daring to look them in the eye, my gaze fell to their stately robes and fine jewelry. They wore incredibly magnificent robes. I hated to admit it, but it was true. I found myself instantly jealous. Why should these savages have robes more luxuriant than mine? Look at the detail of the jewels sewn into the hem! I have never in my life seen anything so majestic. One man had the fur of some kind of animal around his neck and cuffs. Their headwraps had intricately cut gems of every shape and color sewn into the cloth. The gold chains around their necks must have weighed ten pounds. Even their servants were superbly dressed. I hate them more now than when they first came in and ruined my perfectly miserable day.

The magi turned to the side bar and gathered a bit of food from the awaiting trays. They knew that not to imbibe would be insulting in any culture. They sipped the hot drink and ate a little of the food. In a short time four chief

priests and six scholars came bustling into the
room. They had scrolls tucked under their arms.
They had no idea for the reason of their summons.

Then Akbar brought them up to within twenty feet
of me and they bowed low.

I looked down upon them from my throne. I like
how that made me feel superior to my audience.
Looking down my long nose with a slight sneer
traveling over my upper lip as if I had the taste
of a bitter root on the back of my tongue, I
asked the holy men, "Where does your books say
the Christ was to be born?"

The men looked at me, searching their brains for
the answer. They huddled together to confer with
one another. They whispered their debate for a
period of time. One scroll after another was
opened and then closed. Heads shaking in
disagreement, then nodding in affirmation, then
heads scratching in confusion. If I had a sense
of humor, the scene would have made me laugh.

Holy men! I thought to myself. I wanted to spit
out the contempt that I felt for them.

After an insufferable amount of time one priest
seemed to be chosen to act as spokesman.

"Ahem," he cleared his throat as he began. "The

prophet Malachi seems to predict that *'in Bethlehem in Judea,"* He opened the scroll and read, *"'But you, Bethlehem Ephratha, in the land of Judah are by no means least among the rulers of Judah. For from you will come a ruler who will be the shepherd of my people Israel.'"* (Micah 5:2)

I dismissed the holy men.

I then turned to the magi and the interpreter and asked secretly as to the exact time the star had appeared. The interpreter spoke the language of the east and then back to me.

"Appruximaatly two harveests times ago."

"Go to Bethlehem and make careful search for the child," I instructed the interpreter, *"as soon as you find him, report to me so that I too may go and worship him."* (Matthew 2:8) I am such a great liar I snorted to myself. However, the sneer on the corner of my mouth was real.

Worship! HA! Fat chance of that.

The magi received the instructions in good faith and bowed to me and backed out of the room. They

198

were mumbling some gibberish as if I could understand them. I did not try nor did I care what they were trying to say to me. Blah, blah, blah…get out of my kingdom!

"AND GEEZ! COULD SOMEONE DO SOMETHING ABOUT THE SMELL THEY LEFT BEHIND?! CRIMANY, IT SMELLS LIKE A DEAD WET CAMEL AND BURNT FISH IN HERE!"

I stood up and stormed out of the room.

"AKBAR!" Where the heck was that boy? I swear I will beat him for being so incompetent!

"AKBAR! Bring me some food. And bring me a woman!" I was fuming with anger!

"King of the Jews! I am the king of the Jews. No cursed baby is going to take my throne from me!"

"I have to do something to stop that baby!"

I went to my chambers to await some buxom beauty to help me forget my troubles and then fall asleep sweaty and satisfied.

And yet, the nagging thought of one greater than I was born to take my throne ruminated in my brain for months.

LUKE 2:8 – 12 "AND THERE WERE SHEPHERDS LIVING OUT IN THE FIELDS NEARBY, KEEPING WATCH OVER THEIR FLOCKS AT NIGHT. AN ANGEL OF THE LORD APPEARED TO THEM AND THE GLORY OF THE LORD SHONE AROUND THEM AND THEY WERE TERRIFIED. BUT THE ANGEL SAID TO THEM "DO NOT BE AFRAID, I BRING YOU GOOD NEWS OF GREAT JOY THAT WILL BE FOR ALL THE PEOPLE. TODAY IN THE TOWN OF DAVID A SAVIOR HAS BEEN BORN TO YOU; HE IS CHRIST THE LORD.""

21

ISAAC

As the teams of shepherds began to herd their sheep into the folds, I prepared the items with which we would draw lots to see who would take the night watches. I would station three men on three different ridges for three-hour shifts. This valley was a perfectly carved out haven to hold all six of our flocks. It had a natural protective ridge on the north, west and south sides to hem us in safety. The sheepfold was built on the east side where one man would lay across the door to protect the precious cargo stored inside. We all had experience with the wily ways of coyotes, wolves and mountain lions who hunger for mutton. That was why we shepherds spent hours on end honing our skills with our sling shots. We would often have competitions with each other to see who had the most accurate shot, the farthest shot and a host of other games we would make up to man-up one another. Oft times the games got heated and ended with shouting matches and name-calling and accusations of cheating. But boys will be boys and at the end of the day we would head back to our sheep and perform the duty for which we were being paid. After the sheep were secured, we gathered to draw lots for our assignments. I drew the second shift, so I grabbed my bed roll to lie by the fire and catch some sleep knowing that 3AM would come all too soon.

I lay there but sleep eluded me. I wasn't surprised. My thoughts went back to where they had been for two weeks. Estelle or Stella as I like to call her. She is really something. When I am in the village, which is rare these days, I will slip away from my master's farm in the morning when I know she will be at the town well. We talk and laugh. I can only see her eyes through the veil, of course, but I know she is smiling while we talk. Sometimes the wind blows just right and I can smell her scent. It reminds me of some kind of flower I used to smell in my mother's garden. I wish I knew what that flower was.

Her father does not approve. He said I would be nothing more than a shepherd. "Once a low-life shepherd, always a low-life shepherd." But I have dreams. I have ambition. I help out wherever I can and learn as much as I can about running a successful farm. I am getting real good at sheering sheep and can keep the wool in long strands and not short choppy ones. The long strands spin better and make stronger yarn. The women who work with the wool will pay a better price for the long strands. I will work my way out of living in the field watching these sheep and make something of myself.

My father said that I should come and work in the market place with my brothers and him. But I don't want to peddle pots and pans and stuff. I love working with the land and working with animals. I'm not like most of the shepherds that call the sheep 'dumb animals' although I agree they are not the smartest of God's creations. I have seen them eating grass and walk right off the cliff to their death or to severe harm. If a shepherd is not diligent in applying the ointment to their noses, then the sheep could beat their head to their death against a tree or rock seeking relief from the parasites that live in their nasal cavity. That is why being a shepherd is so critical. You must live among the sheep. You must check on each one each day. You must guide them, guard them and watch over them carefully. There are all sorts of dangers lurking to seek and destroy them. I know too many men who do not care for their sheep in this way. They make me sick when I see them mistreating their animals. If I could pick three really great shepherds, we could care for a flock of 500 sheep easily. Give me three good men and we could sheer 500 sheep in a week. I am really good at leading and encouraging men. I hope my master sees that. I hear the other men occasionally speak highly of me. I do hope those words reach the ears of my master.

I hope these words reach the ears of Stella's father. I am more than a shepherd; I am more than just a hired hand. I can make a good living and a good life for his daughter. I love her. Doesn't that account for something? I know that the scripture says that a man must first *'plant his field and then establish his house.'* (Proverbs 24:27) So I plan to speak to my master when we bring in the sheep at the end of the season and ask him where else my services might be used on his farm.

"Please God, help me to improve my lot in life so I can be a good provider for Estelle. Please move in her father's heart that I might find favor in his eyes."

I smiled to myself at the thoughts of Stella. I breathed in deep, trying to remember her scent. I laced my fingers behind my head and gazed up at the stars. Only Stella's beauty can compare to this. The sun had long since cast its tendrils of gold and orange on the ridges to the west to make room for the showcase of jewels in the sky. The sky is black as Stella's hair, and the stars twinkle like her eyes. I do love her. And she is a wonderful cook too.

That was my last thought before I slipped into a dreamless sleep.

I awoke with my heart racing! I thought the bright light was coming from our campfire raging out of control. Jehiel and Zed, who had drawn the lot for 3rd shift with me and were catching some sleep next to the fire with me, were on their feet. Their expression of terror mirrored mine! We looked into the sky from where the bright light was coming. It was so brilliantly white and glorious that we could not take our eyes off of it! We had no idea what it was. It was beautiful, breathtaking and yet masculine, virile, and stately! So many emotions were running through my mind like a swarm of hornets. Terror and fear were chief among the emotions. I could not take my eyes off of the light to look at my friends to see their reactions. The music that seemed to accompany it was pristine and mesmerizing. All of my senses were tingling and on high alert. My heart began to swell with...with...love, with God, with awe and wonder. I actually thought my heart would beat right out of my chest! I could not comprehend what I was seeing! I began to shake. What was this? What was happening?

The natural thing to do I thought was to fall prostrate on my knees. I spent all of my life going to the temple on Sabboth. Papa read from the Torrah, and Mama would tell me and my sisters and brothers stories from of old. I knew God was the God of Israel. I knew we were the apple of His eye. We were chosen by Him to be a royal priesthood, a holy nation just because He loved us.

Jehiel and Zed followed my lead, and we fell to our knees with our faces on the ground. Then we heard the light speak. I lay there and listened and felt that I was in the presence of God. I felt that something very important was about to happen. I sensed that my life was about to change. For some reason the words, "Speak LORD, Your servant is listening," came to my mind.

I muttered the words, "Yes LORD?"

Then the strangest thing happened. The light took shape. Could it be an angel? The angel seemed to look straight at us and said, *"Do not be afraid, I bring you good news of great joy that will be for all the people. Today in the town of David a Savior has been born to you; he is Christ the Lord. This will be a sign to you; you will find a baby wrapped in cloths and lying in a manger."* (Luke 2:10-12)

It was as if the whole heavens exploded into one grand celebration! The sky was lit as bright as day. There were thousands and thousands of angels. At least I think that was what they were. They all seemed to be praising God. The music swelled to a crescendo! I heard trumpets and harps and lyres and cymbals! I have heard beautiful singing before at the temple but it pales in comparison. I lay there letting the music wash over me and through me. I felt myself floating, at least I felt like I was floating. I started humming along. Songs of praise started to rise from my heart too. I didn't know exactly what I was singing, but I just felt like I was worshiping God with this wonderful heavenly host. I still don't know what they were, but they sure were glorious looking.

Suddenly a great company of heavenly host appeared with the angel praising God and saying,

"GLORY TO GOD IN THE HIGHEST AND ON EARTH PEACE AMONG MEN WITH WHOM HE IS PLEASED." (Luke 2:13-14)

And with that, they disappeared. Vanished into the heavens. Harps, trumpets, lyres and all. Gone. Like someone blew out a candle. The world around us returned to its blackness. The campfire seemed like a firefly in comparison. We slowly rose to our feet. The three of us stood there looking into the sky. Our mouths opened like empty caves. No one dared to speak. We did not want to taint the moment with human noises. We wanted to stay drenched in the glory of God for as long as we could. We never wanted this moment to end. I have NEVER felt like this before. I felt like a warm woolen blanket was wrapped around me.

I felt like...I know this sounds crazy, but I felt like I had warm honey poured all over me. The feeling was that heavy.

As much as I hated to, I stole away from looking skyward and turned to Jehiel and Zed. Their eyes slowly lowed back to earth, their mouths finally closed, and they turned to meet my stunned face. No one wanted to be the first to speak and break the moment. We didn't have to. We heard their yelling before we saw them. Shammah, Asahel and Igal came running from their watch posts.

"Jehiel!! Jehiel, Zed! Zed! Isaaaacccc! Man oh Man," the three of them said breathlessly. "YOU GUYS, DID YOU SEE THAT? WHAT WERE THEY?"

All six of us started speaking to each other at once. The excitement was palpable. We felt like school boys who just received new toys! Soon the other three shepherds arrived breathlessly and joined in our excitement.

"What did they mean, 'On earth peace among men with whom He is well pleased?'"

One of us said, "let us go straight to Bethlehem then, and see this thing that has happened which the LORD has made known to us." (Luke 2:15)

Asahel said, "Well, we can't all go, who will stay here with the sheep?"

"Okay," I said, taking control of the situation. "Some of us should go and some need to stay here with the sheep. How about if we go in groups of threes. That way we do not look like a gang walking around Bethlehem seeking out a baby in the middle of the night. Then come back and relieve the ones that stayed."

"Great idea," Sham agreed. "Should we draw lots or can we decide on our own?"

Be a servant leader, I said to myself. "I will stay."

Jehiel said, "I will stay too."

Igal stayed with me and Jehiel, three took off for Bethlehem and the other three went back to their post.

"We will be back as soon as we can," they reassured us.

So they hurried off and found Mary and Joseph and the baby who was lying in the manger. When they had seen him they spread the word concerning what had been told them about this child and all who heard it were amazed at what the shepherds said to them. But Mary treasured up all these things and pondered them in her heart. The shepherds returned glorifying and praising God for all the things they had heard and seen which were just as they had been told. Luke 2:16-20

"WOW! What just happened?" I felt tingly all over. I could hardly wait to see what the LORD had for us! Suddenly Stella's father's disapproval seemed trivial. God sent His messengers to speak to us.

I know that God sees me as valuable.

LUKE 2:25 "AND BEHOLD, THERE WAS A MAN IN JERUSALEM WHOSE NAME WAS SIMEON; AND THIS MAN WAS RIGHTEOUS AND DEVOUT, LOOKING FOR THE CONSOLATION OF ISRAEL AND THE HOLY SPIRIT WAS UPON HIM."

22

SIMEON

I awoke that day feeling odd, like I was forgetting something. Like something was planned that day and I had forgotten about it. I searched my mind as I prepared for the day. I was going to the temple as usual. I didn't recall a festival or feast that was scheduled for that day. I didn't recall making a meeting with anyone. Yet I had a lingering, almost nagging, feeling that something was amiss. After a thorough check of my daily plans, I concluded that indeed I was not forgetting anything important.

"Well, God, I am prepared for anything You will bring my way today. My every breath and my every step belong to you and I know that You counsel me with Your eye."

So after my hearty breakfast I left my home to journey to the temple for my daily service of prayer and worship. It was a remarkable day. Not a cloud in the sky. There was a warm breeze that filled the air with fragrances from the surrounding meadows and gardens. My old bones were cooperating with my movements this morning. Ah yes, it was going to be a spectacular day. I could just feel it.

I walked through the bustling morning market place and stopped to speak to the merchants. I bid shalom to my fellow townsmen and accepted their free samplings of their produce. I wondered sometimes if they took pity upon me as a widower, perhaps thinking that I was unable to cook for myself. I knew they meant well. At the beginning I struggled in the kitchen, but with the many passing years and tips from the wives of my friends, I have become quite adept in the kitchen. I patted my bulging belly as proof.

I did notice that there was a bit more of a buzz in the air, more eager conversation among the townspeople. Then I noticed several shepherds in town. Odd, they are usually in the fields this time of year. Why would they be in town? As I turned the corner towards the temple, I saw a shepherd speaking to one of the priests. That was something you did not see every day. The two diverse social classes were never seen in conversation. This pair seemed to be speaking of something of great importance. The shepherd was very animated in his speech and with arm gestures.

As I made my way to the temple steps, I noticed the priest was my friend Elzaphan. I heard the shepherd say something about an angel visiting them in the fields last week. My old bones caused me to walk slowly up the steps, so I was able to pick up a good bit of their conversation. I stopped alongside Elzaphan to bid him shalom. The two where so engrossed in their conversation that he did not acknowledge me for a few minutes.

"What do you make of this Simeon?" Elzaphan turned to me for my opinion.

"I have no idea of what you speak," I replied.

"This shepherd tells me that several nights ago, an angel visited him and a group of his fellow shepherds while they attended their sheep out in the field. He claims the angel told them that 'the Savior, which is Christ the Lord' was born in Bethlehem that night. He claims that the angel told them that they would find the baby in a barn, of all places. He claims he saw the baby and his parents over in Jake's barn behind his inn."

"IT'S TRUE, IT'S TRUE", the shepherd interrupted Elzaphan. "It was the most marvelous thing we had ever seen! We were scared to death at first, but the angel spoke and told us not to be afraid, and our hearts grew calmer, and then there were hundreds of angels that appeared with the first one all singing praises to God! I will never forget it as long as I live. And sure enough, we ran as fast as we could to Bethlehem. It took a while to look in every barn we could find, because the angel said *this will be a sign for you, you will find a baby wrapped in cloth and laying in a manger.* Now you don't see that everyday. A baby lying in a feeding trough. A brand new baby at that. What were those parents thinking to have a baby in a stinking barn?"

The shepherd was still reminiscing his experience when it struck me! *'A*

Savior is born to you who is Christ the Lord.' Is that what the shepherd said? The Messiah?! God's consolation of Israel? Has it finally come to pass? God had *'revealed to me that I would not see death before I had seen the Lord's Christ.'* (Luke 2:26) Could it finally be true? My heart began to race as I climbed the temple stairs. My old bones feeling more alive than in many years. My heart was racing; I could feel the blood pumping in my ears. How was I going to find this child? How would I recognize Him? If this happened a few days ago, why were the temple priests not made aware of this? Why did God tell shepherds and not tell His priests and temple workers? That seemed a bit unfair. I found myself growing indignant. Why tell some lowly shepherds? Did they even understand what the angel was saying?

I reached the coolness of the temple porch and leaned against the enormous pillar to catch my breath. My body may feel young, but my lungs were still their old selves. I dabbed perspiration from my forehead, straightened my robes and entered the temple. I began to go about my duties when I heard the door open behind me. I turned around and saw a young couple holding a baby.

I heard God say to my spirit, "This is He." As simple as that. I lay down my utensils and walked to the couple. The man had two turtledoves ready for the sacrifice for his baby and wife. I walked slowly to the couple so as not to startle them.

"I know who He is." I slowed my words as much as I could. "He is the long awaited Messiah." The words caught in my throat, and a tear threatened to spill from my eye. I stared at the sleeping baby in His mother's arms. My heart was racing and my mind was spinning with unimaginable joy and praise that I am finally beholding God's promise. I took a deep breath to calm my beating heart and my shaking hands and gathered up the courage to asked the mother, "May I hold Him?"

With as much gentleness as I could muster I reached out my arms and allowed the mother to place God's most precious gift into my arms. I thought my heart would explode! I wanted to dance and shout and run around and show everyone this baby, this fulfillment of scripture!! I could not believe that I was holding the consummation of God's plan of redemption for Israel! He was so tiny!! His little hands, His little nose, His little mouth shaped just like a rose bud. He lay sleeping in my arms, wrapped in a warm blanket.

I did not dance, I did not shout. I actually wanted to drop to my knees in worship. My legs began to shake with emotion. I carefully walked to the side bench to sit down. Holding this baby, I was holding God! I reached my old dried up, crooked hand and touched the baby's warm pink cheek. What a contrast between my knobby knuckles covered in withered skin and the pure radiant skin of a newborn. I have never touched anything so soft and precious. I did not want this moment to end. I let the sting of tears roll out of my eyes. My heart was so full! I could feel the praises of my soul begin to well up within me. I tried to steady my breathing. I began to quietly chant a psalm of old to my God, my Creator, my Redeemer, and my Salvation. *The LORD is faithful to all His promises and loving toward all He has made. The LORD upholds all those who fall and lifts up all who are bowed down. The eyes of all look to You and You give them their food at the proper time. You open Your hand and satisfy the desires of every living thing.* (Psalm 145:13-16)

"Now LORD, thou can let Thy bond-servant depart in peace, according

to Thy word. For my eyes have seen Thy salvation, which Thou hast prepared in the presence of all peoples. A light of revelation to the gentiles and the glory of Thy people Israel." (Luke 2:29-32)

I brought my senses back under control. My heart rejoicing. I handed the baby back to His mother, and being prompted by God I said to her,

"Behold, this Child is appointed for the fall and rise of many in Israel, and for a sign to be opposed and a sword will pierce even your own soul, to the end, that thoughts of many hearts may be revealed." (Luke 2:34-35)

The mother reached down to retrieve her baby from my arms. What warm strong eyes she had. "Thank you, sir," she replied in a hushed tone. She adjusted the tussled baby into the crook of her arm and went back to stand with her husband. They turned towards the priest by the altar to make their sacrifice of purification.

What a marvelously unpredicted day this had turned out to be! The feeling of unsettled angst that I had experienced at the wake of my day had dissipated. It was now replaced with a sense of fulfillment. The long-awaited Messiah, Meshua, had arrived! Praise Be to God, from whom all blessings flow!

I never saw the couple again.

LUKE 2:36- AND THERE WAS A PROPHETESS, ANNA THE DAUGHTER OF PHANUEL, OF THE TRIBE OF ASHER. SHE WAS ADVANCED IN YEARS, HAVING LIVED WITH A HUSBAND SEVEN YEARS AFTER HER MARRIAGE AND THEN AS A WIDOW TILL THE AGE OF EIGHT-FOUR.

23

ANNA

I still remember my wedding day as if it were yesterday, or at least last week. My mother and Nana worked on my wedding gown for months. The embroidery was intricate and very detailed. The lace that my aunt JoAnna made was used in my veil and worked into the bodice. It fit my frame perfectly. The sleeves were long, and flowing and the train was embroidered with little white stones that looked like pearls. No dress of a queen could have looked more beautiful. I could hardly wait to wear it.

I had been betrothed to Ibhar for two years before he finally came for me. Our parents had arranged our marriage while I was still very young. We were very happy about the arrangement. He was so very kind and gentle but strong and worked hard as a farmer. He inherited much land from his father and together with his four brothers had built a marvelous farm. God had blessed the produce of their field and their flocks and herds. Some people called him Abraham because of his many animals and farm hands.

The accident took us all by surprise. My heart catches in my throat every time I think about that fateful day. For years I questioned God. For years I cried out that He was so unfair to take my beloved Ibhar. The priests and my friends tried to comfort me with words from the Torah but I could not bear the loss. For many years I sat alone in my home, in our home. God had not blessed us with children yet, so I was truly alone. We had seven wonderful years together. We desperately wanted to start a family but I was content to do my part on the farm until God smiled upon us with the pitter-patter of little feet.

But in time God spoke to me. God heard my cry. He healed my broken heart and drew me to Himself as my husband. Psalm 34:17-18 became my life verse, *'The righteous cry out and the LORD hears and delivers them out of all their troubles. The LORD is near to the broken hearted and saves those who are crushed in spirit.'* Eventually my spirit began to be less heavy every day. I began to see the beauty in the world around me. Simple things began to give me joy again, the smell of honeysuckle, a child's laugh-a soft spring rain and the smell of fresh cut hay. Then one day I saw a rainbow. I felt God speak to my heart. My mourning was over. God had a new plan for my life. It seemed miraculous. The black cavernous part of my heart filled with unimaginable sorrow was gone like the storm clouds that revealed that rainbow. As I gazed at the rainbow my heart of stone crumbled away and was replaced with a heart of flesh, a heart of peace and hope. I felt myself standing up straight. I actually felt my soul being renewed like a window had just opened up with a breeze blowing through. I felt like I had been given a new birth.

I returned to life again. Friends were so happy to see me visit the market and work among my flowers. I must admit I did have a knack for cultivating God's creations and growing them into marvelous works of beauty to be shared by all. I was given a small home near the temple, and *I served God day and night with prayers and fasting.* (Luke 2:37) And that was where I had been for forty one years. God truly is my husband. He has always wanted to be the husband to Israel but she has rejected Him. I love Him. He is my joy and my ever-present helper. I thank God everyday for allowing me the privilege of serving Him daily.

Today would have been Ibhar and my 66th wedding anniversary. I gladly celebrate it in the service of the God who brought us together as man and wife and blessed us with seven glorious years of marriage.

That was where I was when I saw Simeon speaking to a young couple who had come to the temple with the sacrifice to cleanse the woman who had just given birth. (Leviticus 12:8.) That was when God spoke to my heart. "There is your Salvation."

I waited for the couple to finish with the priest and their sacrifice and met them at the door as they were about to leave. I walked up to the mother and looked her straight in the eyes. I held her gaze for a moment while I tried to contain my composure. "I know Who He is," I whispered excitedly. "May I... may I, hold Him for just a moment?"

The mother graciously held out her arms. The baby was awake and perfectly content. I rearranged the blanket so I could gaze at

His face. The face of God. The face of my Salvation. The face of my Savior, my Messiah. Is this really happening? I held Him to my bosom and let the tears run down my cheeks. I did not want to let Him go. I shut my eyes and found myself rocking gently back and forth, the instinctive way people move when holding a baby. I hummed quietly to my God. My heart would not quiet down. I allowed myself to hold Him for as long as I dare. I opened my eyes and drank in one long look at my Redeemer. I thought my heart would burst with praise! I reluctantly handed Him back to His mother.

"Thank you for letting me hold Him. May God continue to bless you both mightily as you begin your journey to raise this precious gift."

I watched at the doors as they walked down the steps. I *'began giving thanks to God and continued to speak of Him to all those who were looking for the redemption of Jerusalem.'* (Luke 2:38)

With my heart full of adoration for God, I returned to my work in the temple when a thought struck me. I stood up straight as if receiving a marvelous revelation from God! If I had not been a widow, had I not served in the temple day and night, I might have missed this opportunity to see my Savior. An irrepressible smile began to make its way across my face. God's ways are not always our ways. He makes all things work for His glory.

Give thanks to the LORD for He is good, His love endures forever. (Psalm 136:1)

LUKE 2:39 "AND WHEN THEY HAD PERFORMED EVERYTHING ACCORDING TO THE LAW OF THE LORD, THEY RETURNED TO GALILEE, TO THEIR OWN CITY OF NAZARETH

24

MARY

I was so glad to be home. It seemed like we had been gone forever, though we had been gone just over a month. Joseph had prepared our home beautifully before we left. I could not believe I was a wife, a mother and now the woman of a home. How could I be so grown up when I still felt like a little girl inside? I had adjusted to being a mother quickly. It was scary not knowing what to do those first few weeks and not having Mama to teach me. Joseph knew less than I did, but we learned together. We learned what Jesus' different cries meant and we are getting pretty good at this thing called parenting. We will be much more prepared with the next one. Owe vey, am I already talking of more children?

We settled into married and family life easily and quickly. I visited Mama and family often and my siblings played with Jesus and helped him to sit, then crawl and then stand. Now he has been toddling around and getting into everything! I have to be so careful where I lay things because sure enough it will find its way into Jesus' mouth. Did that kid have to taste everything? He was very curious. He seemed to explore every thing. He was a very well-tempered child and the joy of our lives. Joseph could hardly wait to get home from work and play with Him until dinner and then bedtime.

Time passed quickly. I could hardly believe we had just celebrated Jesus' birthday again. We had settled into a comfortable routine of chores, nap, and play and then the high light of Jesus' day... wait outside for daddy to come home! As soon as Joseph would round the corner to our block Jesus would run to him. It was the best part of my day to see Joseph scoop up Jesus and swing him around then hoist him upon his shoulders and carry him home.

One night, we stayed outside to enjoy the twilight when we noticed a commotion coming up the narrow street. It was a caravan of some type. There were several camels lumbering up the street and they seemed to be coming to our house.

The entourage stopped half-way up the street and four riders on their camels dismounted and walked towards our house. Joseph instinctively stepped between them and me and told me to pick up Jesus. The men were elaborately dressed. The colors of their robes were deep and rich, colors I had never seen before. They looked like very prominent men of great means.

The four men stopped twenty feet from us. The smallest of the four and the one not as elaborately dressed as the other three stepped forward to address us.

"Shalom," he said in a very thick accent. "Me neem is Shakara. We huv travled a greet distaunce to find you. Me maastas huv followed bery large star in sky. Star tell us new keeng boorn. Star first take us to smull town culled Beethleehum. No find bubee keeng. Then we see star in nu place. Nort of Beethleehum. We follow star to dis house." Pointing to Jesus Shakara says, "Ez dis bubee king?"

I looked at Joseph in utter disbelief. He returned my shocked look. Joseph nodded and told the man, "Yes, indeed, this is Jesus. He is born the Son of Jehovah God."

A wide smile brightened Shakara's face, revealing perfectly straight white teeth. He bowed and backs away to return to the other three men. He spoke to them in a language that was strange to me. Their excitement grew with every word retold to them. They called to other servants in the entourage who quickly opened up several sacks and retrieved articles from them. The servants brought three packages wrapped in ornately embroidered cloth and handed them to the three 'masters.'

Who were these men? Their clothing spoke of great importance; their eyes showed deep wisdom and yet displayed kindness and adoration. The three men took the packages and unwrapped them and stepped towards Joseph and me. Their scent was like nothing I had ever smelled before. It had a spiciness that seemed to signify authority and power. Chanting in a melodious manner, they each dropped to their knees and bowed prostrate to Jesus. Odd? Do other people worship Jehovah as we do? Do other countries know about the God of Abraham as we do?

After several minutes of the foreign worship to Jesus they came up on one knee and presented the gifts to me. I handed Jesus over to Joseph and stepped toward the men. Shakara stood near us to be ready to interpret. The first gentleman handed me a beautifully carved gold box, richly inlaid with jewels and precious stones. I was thinking the box was the gift. It was the most beautiful thing I had ever seen outside of the Temple.

"Thank you," I said.

Shakara spoke a short phrase to the man. I presume it was

'thank you' in their language. He bowed his head as if he were the one receiving a gift.

I opened the box and nearly dropped it. My mouth and eyes flew open at the same time and surprise filled my lungs. It was filled with gold coins. Roman gold coins.

"Oh my, I cannot accept this!" I said in disbelief. I tried to hand it back.

The ornately dressed man shook his head and pointed to Jesus. "For Keeng," he spoke in broken Hebrew.

I stood holding the chest. The words of my mother quickly came to mind. She always told me to graciously accept any gift or compliment someone would give to you. I paused for a few moments. Tears welling up in my eyes. Not because of the gold but because they called Jesus Keeng, I mean King. These strange men were acknowledging that Jesus is the King of the Jews. How do they know that?

I looked at the man who was still on bended knee before me and smiled my best smile. I bowed to him and said, 'Thank you."

The second master came with his gift and knelt in front of me and extended his arms with an equally exquisite gold box. I drew in my breath, reached for the box and said, "Thank you." I opened the box. It held a bottle full of oil. I held the box open to Joseph and he retrieved the bottle. He opened the top and took a whiff. There was no recognizable expression on his face for several seconds and then his eyes grew wide. He remembered where he had smelled that smell before. It was myrrh. They used it when they buried his mother. Myrrh? Embalming oil? For a baby? For a King? Maybe in their culture they use if for something else, something of great value. Joseph replaced the top of the bottle and laid it back to rest in the golden box. He turned to the second man and said "thank you very much." I set the box on the front stoop next to the first box knowing I had one more gift to receive.

I turned my attention to the third man who stepped forward, bowed to one knee and handed me a third richly-carved and jewel-encrusted box. These men had my curiosity aroused. I smiled and said 'thank you' to the kneeling man and gentle accepted the outstretched box. I could smell the fragrance before I opened the box. Pensively, I opened it. It was filled with the scent that I remembered smelling in the temple. This was the only time I had ever smelled that outside the temple. Why would they have incense that we use for worship? Was it to worship Jesus? These men were incredibly wise. How do they know our customs? These gifts spoke volumes of the strangers' adoration for the King of the Jews. But how? How do they know when our own people do not know?

"Thank you very much," I said to the third man. "Your generosity is overwhelming. The fact that you know that Jesus is born King of the Jews is astounding. Thank you for recognizing Him and worshiping Him."

Shakara repeated my words to the three men and then stepped forward towards Joseph, Jesus and me.

"Thunk you zoo much. We Weer beeginning to geev up hope ov finding zee keeng. Thunk you fur accepteeng geefts from me maastas. We go hume now wit great joy." He continued to bow to us as he backed up to join his masters who had since risen to their feet. I had not noticed how very tall all four gentlemen were until now. They walked backwards to their camels and the rest of their entourage.

The four of them mounted their camels in unison. One gave some sort of command to the rest of the caravan and turned and rode silently out of town.

To say that Joseph and I were stunned to silence is an understatement. We stood together and watched the parade until it was out of sight, and then we watched some more. Had Jesus not squirmed in Joseph's arms, we might have stayed paralyzed all night. Finally we turned to each other.

"What just happened? What in the world was that all about? What do these gifts mean?" All these questions kept coming out of my mouth. Of course, Joseph had no answer. They were his questions, too.

Gold for a king, I understand that. But what kind of gift is myrrh? Frankincense was for the worship of God. That did make sense. We pulled our wits back together and turned to walk inside.

Joseph said, "Well Mawry, leetz take bubee keeng inside."

We both chuckled. We took one more long look down the narrow little street knowing we will never look at it the same way again.

We turned our eyes then to each other, speechless for a moment and then I said, "WOW, that incredible!" We laughed again and then Joseph shifted Jesus in his right arm, wrapped his left around me and ushered me toward our door. I stopped to gently pick up the three boxes from the bench and allowed Joseph to guide me through the door.

Surely this was a night to remember and I treasured all these things in my heart.

MATTHEW 2:13 "AFTER THEY (THE VISITING KINGS) WERE GONE, AN ANGEL OF THE LORD APPEARED TO JOSEPH IN A DREAM. "GET UP, TAKE THE CHILD AND HIS MOTHER AND ESCAPE TO EGYPT. STAY THERE UNTIL I TELL YOU, FOR HEROD IS GOING TO SEARCH FOR THE CHILD TO KILL HIM."

25

JOSEPH

It was so nice to be home again. It was so nice to finally sleep in my own bed. What a whirlwind it has been! The last time I was in this bed, it was the evening when that entourage of noble men brought gifts and worshipped Jesus. Mary and I stayed up very late recounting the evening surprise. I had to admit the gold did come in handy. But we still puzzle over the myrrh and frankincense. How very odd? I'll have to ask Zachariah if there is any significance to those strange gifts.

Mary and I talked well into the night and then finally kissed and said good night. I am not sure how long I had been asleep when an angel appeared in my dream. It seemed to be the same angel as before-the one who told me not to be afraid to take Mary for my wife. Do they all look the same? I have only seen one, so I cannot say for sure. However, this angel did look very much like the first one.

His voice was steady and commanded much authority. He said in a very firm voice filled with urgency. *"Get up, take the child and his mother and escape to Egypt. Stay there until I tell you, for Herod is going to search for the child to kill him."* (Matthew 2:13)

I did not think twice. I did not hesitate. I rolled over and shook Mary firmly. "Mary. Mary. Mary, get up! We must go at once." I quickly tried to explain the dream. She did not think I was mad, but dutifully obeyed and swiftly packed a few necessities. We left while it was still dark. I could feel the angel guiding us. I had only an inkling of the direction toward Egypt. The angel led the way and for a good distance Mary carried Jesus and I led the donkey, which miraculously followed willingly and did not resist.

The trip to Egypt was long and hot. How come we always seem to make these trips when Mary is with child? But she was a trooper and never complained. We had no idea how long we would stay in Egypt. A day turned into a week. A week turned into a month, and then one month ran into another. We found a small place to stay, and I soon found work with other Egyptian carpenters. Their skills were incredible. They did things with wood that I had never seen before. Even though we did not speak the same language, the men were gracious to teach me and helped me earn my keep. Mary too fell into a semblance of routine. She too mentioned learning new cooking techniques from the Egyptian women. Women and children have a natural bond and Mary soon found kindred spirits and playmates for Jesus. The women were very excited to help Mary when it came time to deliver the baby, another boy that we named James. We tried not to get too comfortable in Egypt. We had no idea how long we were to stay so we made the best of the situation.

I did hear a horrible rumor that Herod had murdered all the baby boys under the age of two years old. The news was so terribly disturbing. Had we caused that? Was Herod looking for Jesus? Had all those baby boys perished because Herod was looking to kill Jesus? Those poor babies, those poor mothers. What a monster! I did not tell Mary what I had learned. If she heard the news, it would not be from me.

Then one night the angel came to me again in my dream and said, *"Get up, take the child and his mother and go to the land of Israel for those who were trying to take the child's life are dead."* (Matthew 2:19-20)

I got up the next day and prepared to leave for home. I was pensive in traveling through Judea for fear that Herod's son Archelaus, who was now king, might also seek to do Jesus harm. Again, an angel came to me in my dream and told me to withdraw to the district of Galilee and settle in Nazareth.

So here we are back home. My father and Mary's family had no idea what had happened to us. We left home in the middle of the night after the noble men came, so I am sure they were panicked as to where we had gone. We did not even have time to tell them of the visitors and their strange but wonderful gifts.

This was not exactly what I had in mind when this whole thing started. I love God and am excited that He chose me to raise His Son, but...wow, I wasn't expecting this. But as I reflect on the last several years, all the ups and downs, the hardship as we traveled to Bethlehem originally, having Mary give birth in a stinking barn with all those animals around. Boy, how did she even manage? Then the strange visit from those shepherds. They were so excited and knew that Jesus was something special sent by God Almighty. It was comical to see those earth-hardened boys, dirty and smelly, rough and coarse acting so gentle and polite around the baby. They turned into animated school boys. Big smiles, almost giddy at the idea of seeing 'The Savior who will bring peace to all men."

Then, when we went into the temple for Mary's purification and ran into that older man and woman, they seemed to be expecting Jesus. Everyone seemed surprised but expectant. Then that mind blowing visit from those...men, those kings... those...I still don't know exactly who or what they were. I have never in my life seen anyone so elaborately dressed. Even their camels were draped in stunning cloth and jewels. Who decorates camels? The men's scent was regal too.

I will have to go visit Zechariah and ask him about the strange gifts. Are they a cultural sign of worship or something from God? I wonder what the Torah has to say about all this?

I have to admit it was awfully frightening leaving in the middle of the night for a long strenuous trip to Egypt of all places. I would have never made it without the guiding light of the angel. Or God Himself. I don't know which one it was. I'm not sure it really matters. Why would Herod murder all those babies? What kind of wicked man senselessly wipes out hundreds of children? I do recall a puzzling passage I heard read to me from the Torah. Jeremiah the prophet says something strange, *"A voice is heard in Ramah, weeping and great mourning. Rachel weeping for her children and refusing to be comforted, because they are no more." Jeremiah 31:15.*

After a time in Egypt we were finally home. The boys have settled in and James is old enough to sit and play with Jesus. They seem to be very fond of each other. Jesus is a very good big brother. Mary spent the first several days visiting her mother and catching up with her friends. We are settled again. It feels good. It feels right. We are among the most blessed in Israel. After the unusual start that we have had in God's big plan for our lives, I believe we are ready for anything that might come our way.

I got up to check on the boys one last time. Looking at them sleeping side by side, my heart was filled with overflowing presence of God. To look at Jesus, he looks like any other toddler. He does what all boys do at his age. Run, jump, climb, fall, run, jump, climb, fall...bleed. I wonder what he dreams about? Does God talk to His son in His sleep? I reached down and stroked his hair and ran my rough hands down his cheek. Precious, precious, precious. I leaned over and tuck the blanket up under James' shoulders. I kissed each of them on the tops of their heads and walked back to my bed. I scoot close to Mary and adjust my covers. I lay there for several minutes listening to her rhythmic breathing. God made a good choice in choosing her. She is gentle and compassionate yet tough and stoic. She does not get rattled very easily. She is a very cool headed young lady. I snuggled up close and draped my arm around her.

"Thank You God for all you have done for us. Thank You that You have kept us safe through all the trials that You have sent our way. We trust You with our lives. We are profoundly thankful that You have entrusted us with the raising and nurturing of Your one and only Son. Dear God in heaven, show me how to raise Him. Show me how to be the best possible father to Jesus, James and with whomever You bless us. Especially show me how to be the best husband to Mary. I love her very much. Thank You that You care for our every need."

I paused and let all the indescribable blessings from God run through my mind. My breathing started to mirror

Mary's.

"My life is in Your hands" were my last thoughts.

And I fell asleep.

"And the Child continued to grow and become strong increasing in wisdom; and the grace of God was upon Him." (Luke 2:40)

EPILOG

GOD

For I so loved the world that I sent my only Son that whosoever shall believe in Him may not perish but have everlasting life. I did not send Him into the world to condemn the world but to save the world through Him.[1]

Jesus is the Christ, the Messiah, the Son of the living God. [2]

Here is how it all came about.

I, by wisdom, founded the earth and by understanding I established the heavens. By knowledge the deeps were broken up and the skies dripped with dew.[3] I created the earth and man, Adam, *and put him into the garden of Eden to cultivate it and keep it. I commanded him "From any tree of the garden you may eat freely, but from the tree of the knowledge of good and evil which is in the middle of the garden, you shall not eat, for in the day that you eat from it you shall surely die." Then I fashioned a woman from his rib so he would have a helper suitable for him.*[4]

The woman was deceived by the serpent, the devil, into eating the fruit from the tree of the knowledge of good and evil, and she gave it to her husband who was with her. When I found out *I said to the serpent, "Because you have done this, cursed are you more than all cattle and more than every beast of the field. On your belly shall you go and dust shall you eat all the days of your life. I will put enmity between you and the woman and between your seed and her seed. He shall crush you on the head and you shall bruise him on the heel."*[5]

So just as sin entered the world through one man, and death through sin, and thus, death came to all men because all sinned. For sin came through one man, Adam and death reigned throughout mankind by that one man.[6]

Many years later I found a man named Abram and I said to him, " *Go forth from your relatives and from your father's house to the land which I will show you; and I will make you a great nation, and I will bless you and make your name great; so you shall be a blessing. I will bless those who bless you and the one who curses you I will curse, and in you all the families of the earth shall be blessed.*[7]

By faith Abraham, when he was called, obeyed by going out to a place which he was to receive for an inheritance and he went out not knowing where he was going. By faith he lived as an alien in the land of promise, as in a foreign land, dwelling in tents with Isaac and Jacob, his future sons, fellow heirs of the same promise. Therefore there was born of this man as many descendants as the stars of heaven in number and innumerable as the sand which is by the seashore.[8]

Now when Abram was ninety-nine years old, I appeared to him and said, "I am God Almighty, walk before Me and be blameless. I will establish My covenant between Me, and you and I will multiply you exceedingly. No longer shall your name be called Abram, but your name shall be Abraham. For I will make you the father of a multitude of nations. I will make you exceedingly fruitful, and I will make nations of you, and kings shall come forth from you.[9] *Abraham believed God and it was credited to him as righteousness.*[10]

About 600 years later, *by faith Moses, when he was born was hidden for three months by his parents, because they saw he was a beautiful child and they were not afraid of the king's edict"*[11] that all Hebrew baby boys should be killed. Moses grew up, and later I used him to lead the Hebrew people out of slavery in the land of Egypt.

One day I said to him from Mt. *Sinai 'go down and come up again, you and* (your brother) *Aaron. I gave them ten commandments with which to lead and teach my people. I spoke all these word, saying,*

1. *I am the LORD your God, who brought you out of the land of Egypt, out of the house of slavery. You shall have no other gods before Me.*

2. *You shall not make for yourself an idol, or any likeness of what is in heaven above or on the earth beneath or in the water under the earth. You shall not worship them or serve them.*

3. *You shall not take My name in vain, for I will not leave him unpunished who takes My name in vain.*

4. *Remember the Sabbath day to keep it holy. For in six days I made the heavens and the earth, the sea and all that is in them and rested on the seventh day, therefore I blessed the Sabbath day and made it holy.*

5. *Honor your father and your mother, that your days may be prolonged in the land which I give you.*

6. *You shall not murder.*

7. *You shall not commit adultery.*

8. *You shall not steal.*

9. *You shall not bear false witness against your neighbor.*

10. *You shall not covet your neighbor's house or wife or anything that belongs to your neighbor.*[12]

Then I called to Moses and spoke to him from the tent of meetings saying, " Speak to the sons of Israel and say to them, ' When any man of you brings an offering to the LORD, you shall bring your offering of an animal from the herd or the flock.[13] Thus the priest shall make atonement for him and he shall be forgiven of the sin '"[14] that is still present from Adam. *For this Law*, this sacrificial order of worship, *since it is only a shadow of the good things to come and not the very form of things, can never by the same sacrifices year by year, which they offer continually, make perfect those who bring the sacrifice. Otherwise, would they not have ceased to be offered, because the worshipers, having once been forgiven would no longer have had sins? But in those animal and grain sacrifices there is a reminder of sins year after year. It is impossible for the blood of bulls and goats to take away sin.*[15]

Therefore,

I will make a new covenant with the house of Israel and with the house of Judah. Not like the covenant which I made with their fathers in the day I took them by the hand to bring them out of the land of Egypt, My covenant which they broke, although I was a husband to them. But this is the covenant which I will make with the house of Israel and those who believe upon My Son. *I will put My law within them and on their heart I will write it and I will be their God and they shall be My people. For I will forgive their iniquity and their sin I will remember no more.*"[16]

This is the new covenant.

Zachariah and Elizabeth's son, John, *"continued to grow, and to become strong in spirit and he lived in the deserts until the day of his public appearance to Israel."*[17] *As it is written in Isaiah the prophet, "Behold, I send My messenger before your face who will prepare Your way. The voice of one crying in the wilderness 'Make ready the way of the LORD, make your paths straight."*[18] *John the Baptist appeared in the wilderness preaching a baptism of repentance for the forgiveness of sins. He was preaching and saying, "After me One is coming who is mightier than I, and I am not fit to stoop down and untie the thong of His sandals. I baptized you with water, but He will baptize you with the Holy Spirit."[19]*

When John saw Jesus coming he said, "Behold the Lamb of God who takes away the sins of the world."[20]

Jesus performed many miracles in the presence of His disciples.[21]

When Jesus was about 33 years old, *"He was eating the Passover dinner and reclining at the table with His disciples. While they were eating, Jesus took some bread and after a blessing, He broke it and gave it to the disciples and said "Take, eat, this is My body." And when He had taken a cup and given thanks, He gave it to them saying, 'Drink from it, all of you for this is My blood of the new covenant, which is poured out for many for the forgiveness of sins."[22]*

For if the blood of goats and bulls and the ashes of a heifer will not take away sin, how much more will the blood of Christ cleanse us from dead works to serve Me, the living God?[23] Because without the shedding of blood there is no forgiveness of sins.[24]

"Now the main point in what I have just said is this: you have a new high priest in Jesus, who has taken His seat at the right hand of My throne in heaven. For every high priest is appointed to offer both gifts and sacrifices, hence it is necessary that this High Priest, Jesus, also have something to offer. Jesus is also the mediator of a better covenant, which has been enacted on better

promises. For if that first covenant had been faultless, there would have been no occasion sought for a second.[25] *Therefore the Law has become our tutor to lead us to Christ, that we may be justified by faith."* [26]

For, on the one hand, there is a setting aside of a former commandment because of its weakness and uselessness for the Law made nothing perfect and on the other hand there is a bringing in of a better hope, through which you can now draw near to Me.[27]

Like the high priests of the old covenant who had to daily offer up sacrifices, first for their own sins and then for the sins of the people, Jesus, our new High Priest is holy, innocent, undefiled, separated from sinners and exalted above the heavens. He does not need to bring a daily sacrifice because He did once for all when He offered up Himself. Hence He is able to save forever those of you who draw near to Me through Him, since He always lives to make intercession for you.[28]

Let Me make sure all this is understandable. This is My plan for redeeming mankind from the original sin of Adam.

In the beginning was the Word, and the Word was with Me and the Word was Me. Jesus was with Me in the beginning.[29] *The Word was Me and Jesus, We became flesh and dwelt with mankind on the earth.*[30]

Jesus is Me, I am Jesus. And now Jesus is your great High Priest.

I want you to see that, *"You do not have a high priest who cannot sympathize with your weaknesses, but One who has been tempted in all things as you are, yet without sin. Therefore, you can now draw near with confidence to My throne of grace that you may receive mercy and may find grace to help you in your time of need."*[31]

No one can come to Me except through the atoning blood of Jesus. [32] *Jesus'* death on the cross was what I meant *when I cursed Satan the serpent in the garden of Eden and said that Satan will bruise the heel of the woman's seed but the woman's seed will crush the serpent's* head thus destroying Satan and death.[33] The woman's seed is Jesus.

Jesus was God in the flesh and He came to earth as a baby. *He grew up before God like a tender shoot and like a root out of parched ground; He has no stately form or majesty that we should look upon Him nor appearance that we should be attracted to Him. He was despised and forsaken of men, a man of sorrows and acquainted with grief and like one from whom men hide their face. He was despised and you did not esteem Him. Surely your grief He Himself bore and your sorrows He carried; yet you yourselves esteemed Him stricken, smitten of God and afflicted. But He was pierced through for your transgressions. He was crushed for your iniquities; the chastening of your well being fell upon Him. All of you like sheep have gone astray, each of you have turned to your own way. But I caused the iniquity of mankind to fall on Him. He was oppressed and He was afflicted, yet He did not open His mouth. But I was pleased to crush Him, putting Him to grief, as He would render Himself as a guilt offering, Jesus will see His offspring, He will prolong His days as my good pleasure will prosper in His hand. As a result of the anguish of His soul, I will see it and be satisfied; by My knowledge the Righteous One, Jesus My Servant, will justify the many as He will bear your iniquities.*

Therefore I will allot Him a portion with the great and He will divide the booty with the strong because Jesus poured out Himself to death and was numbered with the transgressors yet He himself bore the sin of many and interceded for the transgressors.[34]

This is why Jesus came to be the Savior of the world-to take the sin of mankind upon His shoulders, die the horrible death of crucifixion, and then rise again to conquer sin and death thus making mankind righteous in My eyes and able to have eternal life in heaven with Me.

Believe the story. Believe My words.

I love you,

Epilog Scripture Reference

1. John 3:16
2. Matthew 16:16
3. Proverbs 3:19
4. Genesis 2:15-20
5. Genesis 3:6-15
6. Romans 5:11-20
7. Genesis 12:1-3
8. Hebrews 11:8-9,12
9. Genesis 17:1-6
10. Hebrews 15:6
11. Hebrews 11:23
12. Exodus 20:1-17
13. Leviticus 1:1-2
14. Leviticus 4:20
15. Hebrews 10:1-4
16. Jeremiah 31:31-34
17. Luke 2:80
18. Isaiah 40:3 & Mark 1:1-3
19. Mark 1:1-4,7,8
20. John 1:29
21. John 20:30
22. Matthew 26:20, 26-28
23. Hebrews 9:13,14
24. Hebrews 9:22
25. Hebrews 8:1,3,6-7
26. Galatians 3:24
27. Hebrews 7:18-19
28. Hebrews 7:25-27
29. John 1:1
30. John 1:14
31. Hebrews 4:15-16
32. John 14:6
33. Genesis 3:15
34. Isaiah 53:2-12

ABOUT THE AUTHOR

Joan (Gebert) Geisler is the 7th of 8 children and raised in a loving home throughout the mid west. Although her parents divorced in 1972 when she was 10 years old, her mother, Helen, prayed fervently and worked hard to provide a stable, supportive home in which to raise the remaining 5 children. Helen had two philosophies by which she lived and instilled them into her children; "If you want it bad enough you will work hard enough for it." and "There is no such thing as can't.'"

Joan had a solid foundation of God, prayer and a strong work ethic on which to build her life. She met Gary on a blind date in March of 1989. He proposed 6 weeks later on bended knee beside the reflecting pool between the Lincoln Memorial and Washington Monument in Washington DC. They married in August and have lived happily ever after in Fredericksburg, Virginia, "The most historic town in America."

Look for future books by Joan M. Geisler.

You may think you know the story of Noah's Arc, but did you know that Noah, his wife, their three sons, Shem, Ham and Japeth and their three wives were on the Arc for more than one year? Can you imagine three daughter-in-laws and a mother-in-law cooped up together? With all of the animals to feed and dung to shovel! Now that's a story! The working title of Joan's next book is: <u>"The Real Housewives of Noah's Arc"</u>

Also, Joan and Gary have been working on a parenting book. A fun and whimsical yet profound book that translates metaphors and parables of sporting rules, regulations, strategies and terminologies into practical parenting tips and advice. This book is for the sports enthusiast and those who just need a little comic relief from parenting. The working title for this book is: <u>"All 'Bout Team."</u>

Made in the USA
Charleston, SC
10 October 2013